Learning Reactive Programming with Java 8

Learn how to use RxJava and its reactive Observables to build fast, concurrent, and powerful applications through detailed examples

Nickolay Tsvetinov

BIRMINGHAM - MUMBAI

Learning Reactive Programming with Java 8

First published: June 2015

Production reference: 1170615

Published by Packt Publishing Ltd.
Livery Place
35 Livery Street
Birmingham B3 2PB, UK.

ISBN 978-1-78528-872-2

www.packtpub.com

Credits

Author
Nickolay Tsvetinov

Reviewers
Samuel Gruetter
Dávid Karnok
Timo Tuominen
Shixiong Zhu

Commissioning Editor
Veena Pagare

Acquisition Editor
Larrisa Pinto

Content Development Editor
Adrian Raposo

Technical Editor
Abhishek R. Kotian

Copy Editors
Brandt D'mello
Neha Vyas

Project Coordinator
Sanchita Mandal

Proofreader
Safis Editing

Indexer
Mariammal Chettiyar

Production Coordinator
Conidon Miranda

Cover Work
Conidon Miranda

About the Author

Nickolay Tsvetinov is a professional all-round web developer at TransportAPI — Britain's first comprehensive open platform for transport solutions. During his career as a software developer, he experienced both good and bad and played with most of the popular programming languages — from C and Java to Ruby and JavaScript. For the last 3-4 years, he's been creating and maintaining single-page applications (SPA) and the backend API architectures that serve them. He is a fan of open source software, Rails, Vim, Sinatra, Ember.js, Node. js, and Nintendo. He was an unsuccessful musician and poet, but he is a successful husband and father. His area of interest and expertise includes the declarative/ functional and reactive programming that resulted in the creation of ProAct.js (`http://proactjs.com`), which is a library that augments the JavaScript language and turns it into a reactive language.

First of all, I want to thank my wife, Tanya. I wrote this book because she told me that I was capable of doing this. She was with me all these months; I worked late at night and on weekends, but she didn't mind that. She also helped me with the content of this book. Thank you, Tanya; I love you and I dedicate this book to you. I want to thank my baby girl, Dalia. She is the one who makes me learn and do new things. One day, I want her to be proud of me — she is my sun. I want to thank my colleagues from TransportAPI, especially Dave, who helped me with my English, and Jonathan and Martin, who gave me the courage to finish the book.

I want to thank Astea Solutions, as they gave me space to write, as well as my parents, Georgi and Dimana, who did the same for me on weekends. Finally, I want to thank all my friends who supported me — Simeon, Rosen, Deyan, Pavel, my sister, Marina, and many more.

Thank you!

About the Reviewers

Samuel Gruetter holds a BSc degree in computer science from École Polytechnique Fédérale de Lausanne (EPFL), Switzerland. As a student assistant and member of the Scala team at EPFL, he developed RxScala, which is a Scala adaptor for the RxJava Reactive Extensions library. In this way, he contributed to RxJava. He was also a teaching assistant for the *Principles of Reactive Programming* massive open online course on Coursera, which is the first online course on reactive programming.

Dávid Karnok is a research assistant and PhD student at the Research Laboratory on Engineering and Management Intelligence of the Institute for Computer Science and Control of the Hungarian Academy of Sciences.

He has been working with Java and related core technologies since 2005 to bring Java's benefits to manufacturing and logistic companies.

He was the first to port Microsoft's Rx.NET framework to Java back in 2010; however, the concept was so ahead of its time that his library didn't catch much attention until Netflix came out with the independent RxJava port in 2013. He joined the project not much later and is a core collaborator and has contributed to about 30 percent of the code in the library over the years. With several years of reactive programming experience and as a core developer of RxJava, he frequently answers questions about the library on Stack Overflow, where he reviews pull requests on the RxJava GitHub project page and posts bug fixes and enhancements on a regular basis.

Timo Tuominen develops large-scale software projects from conception to completion for clients, including major telcos and device manufacturers. As the technical lead, he has created dozens of products and services both for consumer and business use.

Working with Futurice, he started using RxJava in 2013 and designed one of the first pure RxJava architectures on Android. His novel approach was a result of the uncompromising functional reactive programming principles that he applied to an existing platform. Several apps and thousands of code commits later, he is now convinced that RxJava and FRP represent a new and better way to build software.

I would like to dedicate this book to everyone who has put up with my RxJava innovations.

Shixiong Zhu is an RxJava committer and also maintains the RxScala project. He received his master's of science degree in computer science from Peking University, China. After that, he joined MicroStrategy and worked on several big data projects. He has also worked on the infrastructure team at Xiaomi. Currently, he is living in Beijing and working on the Apache Spark project, which is a fast and general platform for large-scale data processing.

www.PacktPub.com

Support files, eBooks, discount offers, and more

For support files and downloads related to your book, please visit www.PacktPub.com.

Did you know that Packt offers eBook versions of every book published, with PDF and ePub files available? You can upgrade to the eBook version at www.PacktPub.com and as a print book customer, you are entitled to a discount on the eBook copy. Get in touch with us at service@packtpub.com for more details.

At www.PacktPub.com, you can also read a collection of free technical articles, sign up for a range of free newsletters and receive exclusive discounts and offers on Packt books and eBooks.

https://www2.packtpub.com/books/subscription/packtlib

Do you need instant solutions to your IT questions? PacktLib is Packt's online digital book library. Here, you can search, access, and read Packt's entire library of books.

Why subscribe?

- Fully searchable across every book published by Packt
- Copy and paste, print, and bookmark content
- On demand and accessible via a web browser

Free access for Packt account holders

If you have an account with Packt at www.PacktPub.com, you can use this to access PacktLib today and view 9 entirely free books. Simply use your login credentials for immediate access.

Table of Contents

Preface

Reactive programming has been around for decades. There has been a few implementations of reactive programming from the time Smalltalk was a young language. However, it has only become popular recently and it is now becoming a trend. Why now you ask? Because it is good for writing fast, real-time applications and current technologies and the Web demand this.

I got involved in it back in 2008, when the team I was part of was developing a multimedia book creator called Sophie 2. It had to be fast and responsive so we created a framework called Prolib, which provided objects with properties which could depend on each other (in other words, we implemented bindings for Swing and much more—transformations, filtering, and so on). It felt natural to wire the model data to the GUI like this.

Of course, this was far away from the functional-like approach that comes with RX. In 2010, Microsoft released RX and, after that, Netflix ported it to Java—RxJava. However, Netflix released RxJava to the open source community and the project became a huge success. Many other languages have their port of RX and many alternatives to it. Now, you can code using reactive programming on your Java backend and wire it to your RxJava's frontend.

This book tries to explain to you what reactive programming is all about and how to use it with RxJava. It has many small examples and it explains concepts and API details in small steps. After reading this book, you will have an idea of RxJava, functional programming, and the reactive paradigm.

What this book covers

Chapter 1, An Introduction to Reactive Programming, will introduce you to the concept of reactive programming and will tell you why you should learn about it. This chapter contains examples that demonstrate how RxJava incorporates the reactive programming concept.

Chapter 2, Using the Functional Constructions of Java 8, will teach you how to use the new lambda constructions of Java 8. It will explain some functional programming concepts and will show you how to use them with RxJava in your reactive programs.

Chapter 3, Creating and Connecting Observables, Observers, and Subjects, will show you the basic building blocks of the RxJava library called the Observables. You will learn the difference between 'hot' and 'cold' Observables and how to subscribe to and unsubscribe from them using a subscription instance.

Chapter 4, Transforming, Filtering, and Accumulating Your Data, will walk you through the basic reactive operators, which you will learn how to use to achieve step-by-step computations. This chapter will give you an idea of how to transform the events the Observables emit, how to filter only the data we need, and how to group, accumulate, and process it.

Chapter 5, Combinators, Conditionals, and Error Handling, will present you with more complex reactive operators, which will allow you to master observable chaining. You will learn about the combining and conditional operators and how the Observables interact with each other. This chapter demonstrates the different approaches to error handling.

Chapter 6, Using Concurrency and Parallelism with Schedulers, will guide you through the process of writing concurrent and parallel programs with RxJava. This will be accomplished by the RxJava Schedulers. The types of Schedulers will be introduced and you will come to know when and why to use each one of them. This chapter will present you with a mechanism that will show you how to avoid and apply backpressure.

Chapter 7, Testing Your RxJava Application, will show you how to unit test your RxJava applications.

Chapter 8, Resource Management and Extending RxJava, will teach you how to manage the resources used as data sources by your RxJava applications. We will write our own Observable operators here.

What you need for this book

In order to run the examples, you will need:

- Java 8 installed, which you can download from Oracle's site `http://www.oracle.com/technetwork/java/javase/downloads/jdk8-downloads-2133151.html`

- Gradle to build the project—2.x, which you can download from `https://gradle.org/downloads`

- Eclipse to open the project. You will also need the Gradle plugin for Eclipse, which can be downloaded from the Eclipse MarketPlace. Of course, you can use Gradle from the command line and go through the code with Vim or any other arbitrary text editor

Who this book is for

If you are a Java developer who knows how to write software and would like to learn how to apply your existing skills to reactive programming, this book is for you.

This book can be helpful to anybody no matter if they are beginners, advanced programmers, or even experts. You don't need to have any experience with either Java 8's lambdas and streams or with RxJava.

Conventions

In this book, you will find a number of text styles that distinguish between different kinds of information. Here are some examples of these styles and an explanation of their meaning.

Code words in text, database table names, folder names, filenames, file extensions, pathnames, dummy URLs, user input, and Twitter handles are shown as follows: "We can include other contexts through the use of the `include` directive."

A block of code is set as follows:

```
Observable
  .just('R', 'x', 'J', 'a', 'v', 'a')
  .subscribe(
    System.out::print,
    System.err::println,
    System.out::println
  );
```

When we wish to draw your attention to a particular part of a code block, the relevant lines or items are set in bold:

```
Observable<Object> obs = Observable
  .interval(40L, TimeUnit.MILLISECONDS)
  .switchMap(v ->
    Observable
      .timer(0L, 10L, TimeUnit.MILLISECONDS)
      .map(u -> "Observable <" + (v + 1) + "> : " + (v + u)))
  );
subscribePrint(obs, "switchMap");
```

New terms and **important words** are shown in bold. Words that you see on the screen, for example, in menus or dialog boxes, appear in the text like this: "Interfaces of this type are called **functional interfaces**."

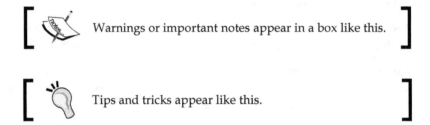

Warnings or important notes appear in a box like this.

Tips and tricks appear like this.

Reader feedback

Feedback from our readers is always welcome. Let us know what you think about this book—what you liked or disliked. Reader feedback is important for us as it helps us develop titles that you will really get the most out of.

To send us general feedback, simply e-mail feedback@packtpub.com, and mention the book's title in the subject of your message.

If there is a topic that you have expertise in and you are interested in either writing or contributing to a book, see our author guide at www.packtpub.com/authors.

Customer support

Now that you are the proud owner of a Packt book, we have a number of things to help you to get the most from your purchase.

Downloading the example code

You can download the example code files from your account at http://www.packtpub.com for all the Packt Publishing books you have purchased. If you purchased this book elsewhere, you can visit http://www.packtpub.com/support and register to have the files e-mailed directly to you.

Errata

Although we have taken every care to ensure the accuracy of our content, mistakes do happen. If you find a mistake in one of our books—maybe a mistake in the text or the code—we would be grateful if you could report this to us. By doing so, you can save other readers from frustration and help us improve subsequent versions of this book. If you find any errata, please report them by visiting http://www.packtpub.com/submit-errata, selecting your book, clicking on the **Errata Submission Form** link, and entering the details of your errata. Once your errata are verified, your submission will be accepted and the errata will be uploaded to our website or added to any list of existing errata under the Errata section of that title.

To view the previously submitted errata, go to https://www.packtpub.com/books/content/support and enter the name of the book in the search field. The required information will appear under the **Errata** section.

Piracy

Piracy of copyrighted material on the Internet is an ongoing problem across all media. At Packt, we take the protection of our copyright and licenses very seriously. If you come across any illegal copies of our works in any form on the Internet, please provide us with the location address or website name immediately so that we can pursue a remedy.

Please contact us at copyright@packtpub.com with a link to the suspected pirated material.

We appreciate your help in protecting our authors and our ability to bring you valuable content.

Questions

If you have a problem with any aspect of this book, you can contact us at questions@packtpub.com, and we will do our best to address the problem.

1
An Introduction to Reactive Programming

Nowadays, the term **reactive programming** is trending. Libraries and frameworks in various programming languages are emerging. Blog posts, articles and presentations about reactive programming are being created. Big companies, such as Facebook, SoundCloud, Microsoft, and Netflix, are supporting and using this concept. So we, as programmers, are starting to wonder about it. Why are people so excited about reactive programming? What does it mean to be reactive? Would it be helpful in our projects? Should we learn how to use it?

Meanwhile, Java is popular with its multi-threading, speed, reliability, and good portability. It is used for building a wide variety of applications, from search engines, through databases to complex web applications running on server clusters. But Java has bad reputation too—it is very hard to write both concurrent and simple applications using only the built-in tools, and programming in Java requires writing a lot of boilerplate code. Also, if you need to be asynchronous (using futures, for example), you can easily get into "callback hell", which actually holds true for all programming languages.

In other words, Java is powerful and you can create great applications with it, but it won't be easy. The good news is that there is a way to change that, using the reactive style of programming.

This book will present **RxJava** (`https://github.com/ReactiveX/RxJava`), an open source Java implementation of the reactive programming paradigm. Writing code using RxJava requires a different kind of thinking, but it will give you the power to create complex logic using simple pieces of well-structured code.

In this chapter, we will cover:

- What reactive programming is
- Reasons to learn and use this style of programming
- Setting up RxJava and comparing it with familiar patterns and structures
- A simple example with RxJava

What is reactive programming?

Reactive programming is a paradigm that revolves around the propagation of change. In other words, if a program propagates all the changes that modify its data to all the interested parties (users, other programs, components, and subparts), then this program can be called **reactive**.

A simple example of this is Microsoft Excel. If you set a number in cell A1 and another number in cell 'B1', and set cell 'C1' to SUM(A1, B1); whenever 'A1' or 'B1' changes, 'C1' will be updated to be their sum.

Let's call this **the reactive sum**.

What is the difference between assigning a simple variable c to be equal to the sum of the a and b variables and the reactive sum approach?

In a normal Java program, when we change 'a' or 'b', we will have to update 'c' ourselves. In other words, the change in the flow of the data represented by 'a' and 'b', is not propagated to 'c'. Here is this illustrated through source code:

```
int a = 4;
int b = 5;
int c = a + b;
System.out.println(c); // 9

a = 6;
System.out.println(c);
// 9 again, but if 'c' was tracking the changes of 'a' and 'b',
// it would've been 6 + 5 = 11
```

Downloading the example code

You can download the example code files for all Packt books you have purchased from your account at http://www.packtpub.com. If you purchased this book elsewhere, you can visit http://www.packtpub.com/support and register to have the files e-mailed directly to you.

This is a very simple explanation of what "being reactive" means. Of course, there are various implementations of this idea and there are various problems that these implementations must solve.

Why should we be reactive?

The easiest way for us to answer this question is to think about the requirements we have while building applications these days.

While 10-15 years ago it was normal for websites to go through maintenance or to have a slow response time, today everything should be online 24/7 and should respond with lightning speed; if it's slow or down, users would prefer an alternative service. Today slow means unusable or broken. We are working with greater volumes of data that we need to serve and process fast.

HTTP failures weren't something rare in the recent past, but now, we have to be fault-tolerant and give our users readable and reasonable message updates.

In the past, we wrote simple desktop applications, but today we write web applications, which should be fast and responsive. In most cases, these applications communicate with a large number of remote services.

These are the new requirements we have to fulfill if we want our software to be competitive. So in other words we have to be:

- Modular/dynamic: This way, we will be able to have 24/7 systems, because modules can go offline and come online without breaking or halting the entire system. Additionally, this helps us better structure our applications as they grow larger and manage their code base.
- Scalable: This way, we are going to be able to handle a huge amount of data or large numbers of user requests.
- Fault-tolerant: This way, the system will appear stable to its users.
- Responsive: This means fast and available.

Let's think about how to accomplish this:

- We can become modular if our system is *event-driven*. We can divide the system into multiple micro-services/components/modules that are going to communicate with each other using notifications. This way, we are going to react to the data flow of the system, represented by notifications.
- To be scalable means to react to the ever-growing data, to react to load without falling apart.

- Reacting to failures/errors will make the system more fault-tolerant.
- To be responsive means reacting to user activity in a timely manner.

If the application is event-driven, it can be decoupled into multiple self-contained components. This helps us become more scalable, because we can always add new components or remove old ones without stopping or breaking the system. If errors and failures are passed to the right component, which can handle them as notifications, the application can become more fault-tolerant or resilient. So if we build our system to be event-driven, we can more easily achieve scalability and failure tolerance, and a scalable, decoupled, and error-proof application is fast and responsive to users.

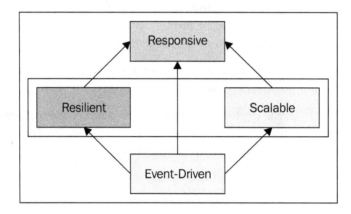

The **Reactive Manifesto** (http://www.reactivemanifesto.org/) is a document defining the four reactive principles that we mentioned previously. Each reactive system should be message-driven (event-driven). That way, it can become loosely coupled and therefore scalable and resilient (fault-tolerant), which means it is reliable and responsive (see the preceding diagram).

Note that the Reactive Manifesto describes a reactive system and is not the same as our definition of reactive programming. You can build a message-driven, resilient, scalable, and responsive application without using a reactive library or language.

Changes in the application data can be modeled with notifications, which can be propagated to the right handlers. So, writing applications using reactive programming is the easiest way to comply with the Manifesto.

Introducing RxJava

To write reactive programs, we need a library or a specific programming language, because building something like that ourselves is quite a difficult task. Java is not really a reactive programming language (it provides some tools like the `java.util.Observable` class, but they are quite limited). It is a statically typed, object-oriented language, and we write a lot of boilerplate code to accomplish simple things (POJOs, for example). But there are reactive libraries in Java that we can use. In this book, we will be using RxJava (developed by people in the Java open source community, guided by Netflix).

Downloading and setting up RxJava

You can download and build RxJava from Github (`https://github.com/ReactiveX/RxJava`). It requires zero dependencies and supports Java 8 lambdas. The documentation provided by its Javadoc and the GitHub wiki pages is well structured and some of the best out there. Here is how to check out the project and run the build:

```
$ git clone git@github.com:ReactiveX/RxJava.git
$ cd RxJava/
$ ./gradlew build
```

Of course, you can also download the prebuilt JAR. For this book, we'll be using version 1.0.8.

If you use Maven, you can add RxJava as a dependency to your `pom.xml` file:

```
<dependency>
  <groupId>io.reactivex</groupId>
  <artifactId>rxjava</artifactId>
  <version>1.0.8</version>
</dependency>
```

Alternatively, for Apache Ivy, put this snippet in your Ivy file's dependencies:

```
<dependency org="io.reactivex" name="rxjava" rev="1.0.8" />
```

If you use Gradle instead, update your `build.gradle` file's dependencies as follows:

```
dependencies {
  ...
  compile 'io.reactivex:rxjava:1.0.8'
  ...
}
```

The code examples and programs accompanying this book can be built and tested with Gradle. It can be downloaded from this Github repository: `https://github.com/meddle0x53/learning-rxjava`.

Now, let's take a peek at what RxJava is all about. We are going to begin with something well known, and gradually get into the library's secrets.

Comparing the iterator pattern and the RxJava Observable

As a Java programmer, it is highly possible that you've heard or used the `Iterator` pattern. The idea is simple: an `Iterator` instance is used to traverse through a container (collection/data source/generator), pulling the container's elements one by one when they are required, until it reaches the container's end. Here is a little example of how it is used in Java:

```
List<String> list = Arrays.asList("One", "Two", "Three", "Four",
"Five"); // (1)

Iterator<String> iterator = list.iterator(); // (2)

while(iterator.hasNext()) { // 3
  // Prints elements (4)
  System.out.println(iterator.next());
}
```

Every `java.util.Collection` object is an `Iterable` instance which means that it has the method `iterator()`. This method creates an `Iterator` instance, which has as its source the collection. Let's look at what the preceding code does:

1. We create a new `List` instance containing five strings.

2. We create an `Iterator` instance from this `List` instance, using the `iterator()` method.

3. The `Iterator` interface has two important methods: `hasNext()` and `next()`. The `hasNext()` method is used to check whether the `Iterator` instance has more elements for traversing. Here, we haven't begun going through the elements, so it will return `True`. When we go through the five strings, it will return `False` and the program will proceed after the `while` loop.

4. The first five times, when we call the `next()` method on the `Iterator` instance, it will return the elements in the order they were inserted in the collection. So the strings will be printed.

In this example, our program consumes the items from the `List` instance using the `Iterator` instance. It pulls the data (here, represented by strings) and the current thread blocks until the requested data is ready and received. So, for example, if the `Iterator` instance was firing a request to a web server on every `next()` method call, the main thread of our program would be blocked while waiting for each of the responses to arrive.

RxJava's building blocks are the observables. The `Observable` class (note that this is not the `java.util.Observable` class that comes with the JDK) is the mathematical dual of the `Iterator` class, which basically means that they are like the two sides of the same coin. It has an underlying collection or computation that produces values that can be consumed by a consumer. But the difference is that the consumer doesn't "pull" these values from the producer like in the `Iterator` pattern. It is exactly the opposite; the producer 'pushes' the values as notifications to the consumer.

Here is an example of the same program but written using an `Observable` instance:

```
List<String> list = Arrays.asList("One", "Two", "Three", "Four",
"Five"); // (1)

Observable<String> observable = Observable.from(list); // (2)

observable.subscribe(new Action1<String>() { // (3)
  @Override
  public void call(String element) {
    System.out.println(element); // Prints the element (4)
  }
});
```

Here is what is happening in the code:

1. We create the list of strings in the same way as in the previous example.

2. Then, we create an `Observable` instance from the list, using the `from(Iterable<? extends T> iterable)` method. This method is used to create instances of `Observable` that send all the values synchronously from an `Iterable` instance (the list in our case) one by one to their subscribers (consumers). We'll look at how the values are sent to the subscribers one by one in *Chapter 3, Creating and Connecting Observables, Observers, and Subjects.*

3. Here, we can subscribe to the Observable instance. By subscribing, we tell RxJava that we are interested in this Observable instance and want to receive notifications from it. We subscribe using an anonymous class implementing the Action1 interface, by defining a single method — call(T). This method will be called by the Observable instance every time it has a value, ready to be pushed. Always creating new Action1 instances may seem too verbose, but Java 8 solves this verbosity. We'll learn more about that in *Chapter 2, Using the Functional Constructions of Java 8.*

4. So, every string from the source list will be pushed through to the call() method, and it will be printed.

Instances of the RxJava Observable class behave somewhat like asynchronous iterators, which notify that there is a next value their subscribers/consumers by themselves. In fact, the Observable class adds to the classic Observer pattern (implemented in Java — see java.util.Observable, see Design Patterns: Elements of Reusable Object-Oriented Software by the Gang Of Four) two things available in the Iterable type.

- The ability to signal the consumer that there is no more data available. Instead of calling the hasNext() method, we can attach a subscriber to listen for a 'OnCompleted' notification.

- The ability to signal the subscriber that an error has occurred. Instead of try-catching an error, we can attach an error listener to the Observable instance.

These listeners can be attached using the subscribe(Action1<? super T>, Action1 <Throwable>, Action0) method. Let's expand the Observable instance example by adding error and completed listeners:

```
List<String> list = Arrays.asList("One", "Two", "Three", "Four",
"Five");

Observable<String> observable = Observable.from(list);
observable.subscribe(new Action1<String>() {
  @Override
  public void call(String element) {
    System.out.println(element);
  }
},
new Action1<Throwable>() {
  @Override
  public void call(Throwable t) {
    System.err.println(t); // (1)
  }
},
```

```
new Action0() {
  @Override
  public void call() {
    System.out.println("We've finnished!"); // (2)
  }
});
```

The new things here are:

1. If there is an error while processing the elements, the `Observable` instance will send this error through the `call(Throwable)` method of this listener. This is analogous to the try-catch block in the `Iterator` instance example.

2. When everything finishes, this `call()` method will be invoked by the `Observable` instance. This is analogous to using the `hasNext()` method in order to see if the traversal over the `Iterable` instance has finished and printing "We've finished!".

 This example is available at GitHub and can be viewed/downloaded at https://github.com/meddle0x53/learning-rxjava/blob/master/src/main/java/com/packtpub/reactive/chapter01/ObservableVSIterator.java.

We saw how we can use the `Observable` instances and that they are not so different from something familiar to us—the `Iterator` instance. These `Observable` instances can be used for building asynchronous streams and pushing data updates to their subscribers (they can have multiple subscribers).This is an implementation of the reactive programming paradigm. The data is being propagated to all the interested parties—the subscribers.

Coding using such streams is a more functional-like implementation of Reactive Programming. Of course, there are formal definitions and complex terms for it, but this is the simplest explanation.

Subscribing to events should be familiar; for example, clicking on a button in a GUI application fires an event which is propagated to the subscribers—handlers. But, using RxJava, we can create data streams from anything—file input, sockets, responses, variables, caches, user inputs, and so on. On top of that, consumers can be notified that the stream is closed, or that there has been an error. So, by using these streams, our applications can react to failure.

To summarize, a stream is a sequence of ongoing messages/events, ordered as they are processed in real time. It can be looked at as a value that is changing through time, and these changes can be observed by subscribers (consumers), dependent on it. So, going back to the example from Excel, we have effectively replaced the traditional variables with "reactive variables" or RxJava's `Observable` instances.

Implementing the reactive sum

Now that we are familiar with the `Observable` class and the idea of how to use it to code in a reactive way, we are ready to implement the reactive sum, mentioned at the beginning of this chapter.

Let's look at the requirements our program must fulfill:

- It will be an application that runs in the terminal.

- Once started, it will run until the user enters `exit`.

- If the user enters `a:<number>`, the *a* collector will be updated to the *<number>*.

- If the user enters `b:<number>`, the *b* collector will be updated to the *<number>*.

- If the user enters anything else, it will be skipped.

- When both the *a* and *b* collectors have initial values, their sum will automatically be computed and printed on the standard output in the format *a + b = <sum>*. On every change in *a* or *b*, the sum will be updated and printed.

The source code contains features that we will discuss in detail in the next four chapters.

The first piece of code represents the main body of the program:

```
ConnectableObservable<String> input = from(System.in); // (1)

Observable<Double> a = varStream("a", input); (2)
Observable<Double> b = varStream("b", input);

ReactiveSum sum = new ReactiveSum(a, b); (3)

input.connect(); (4)
```

There are a lot of new things happening here:

1. The first thing we must do is to create an `Observable` instance, representing the standard input stream (`System.in`). So, we use the `from(InputStream)` method (implementation will be presented in the next code snippet) to create a `ConnectableObservable` variable from the `System.in`. The `ConnectableObservable` variable is an `Observable` instance and starts emitting events coming from its source only after its `connect()` method is called. Read more on it in *Chapter 3*, *Creating and Connecting Observables, Observers, and Subjects*.

2. We create two `Observable` instances representing the a and b values, using the `varStream(String, Observable)` method, which we are going to examine later. The source stream for these values is the input stream.

3. We create a `ReactiveSum` instance, dependent on the a and b values.

4. And now, we can start listening to the input stream.

This code is responsible for building dependencies in the program and starting it off. The a and b values are dependent on the user input and their sum is dependent on them.

Now let's look at the implementation of the `from(InputStream)` method, which creates an `Observable` instance with the `java.io.InputStream` source:

```
static ConnectableObservable<String> from(final InputStream
stream) {
  return from(new BufferedReader(new InputStreamReader(stream)));
  // (1)
}

static ConnectableObservable<String> from(final BufferedReader
reader) {
  return Observable.create(new OnSubscribe<String>() { // (2)
    @Override
    public void call(Subscriber<? super String> subscriber) {
      if (subscriber.isUnsubscribed()) {  // (3)
        return;
      }
      try {
        String line;
        while(!subscriber.isUnsubscribed() &&
          (line = reader.readLine()) != null) { // (4)
            if (line == null || line.equals("exit")) { // (5)
              break;
            }
```

```
              subscriber.onNext(line); // (6)
          }
      }
      catch (IOException e) { // (7)
        subscriber.onError(e);
      }
      if (!subscriber.isUnsubscribed()) // (8)
      subscriber.onCompleted();
    }
  }
}).publish(); // (9)
}
```

This is one complex piece of code, so let's look at it step-by-step:

1. This method implementation converts its InputStream parameter to the BufferedReader object and to calls the from(BufferedReader) method. We are doing that because we are going to use strings as data, and working with the Reader instance is easier.

2. So the actual implementation is in the second method. It returns an Observable instance, created using the Observable.create(OnSubscribe) method. This method is the one we are going to use the most in this book. It is used to create Observable instances with custom behavior. The rx.Observable.OnSubscribe interface passed to it has one method, call(Subscriber). This method is used to implement the behavior of the Observable instance because the Subscriber instance passed to it can be used to emit messages to the Observable instance's subscriber. A subscriber is the client of an Observable instance, which consumes its notifications. Read more about that in *Chapter 3, Creating and Connecting Observables, Observers, and Subjects*.

3. If the subscriber has already unsubscribed from this Observable instance, nothing should be done.

4. The main logic is to listen for user input, while the subscriber is subscribed. Every line the user enters in the terminal is treated as a message. This is the main loop of the program.

5. If the user enters the word exit and hits *Enter*, the main loop stops.

6. Otherwise, the message the user entered is passed as a notification to the subscriber of the Observable instance, using the onNext(T) method. This way, we pass everything to the interested parties. It's their job to filter out and transform the raw messages.

7. If there is an IO error, the subscribers are notified with an OnError notification through the onError(Throwable) method.

8. If the program reaches here (through breaking out of the main loop) and the subscriber is still subscribed to the `Observable` instance, an `OnCompleted` notification is sent to the subscribers using the `onCompleted()` method.

9. With the `publish()` method, we turn the new `Observable` instance into `ConnectableObservable` instance. We have to do this because, otherwise, for every subscription to this `Observable` instance, our logic will be executed from the beginning. In our case, we want to execute it only once and all the subscribers to receive the same notifications; this is achievable with the use of a `ConnectableObservable` instance. Read more about that in *Chapter 3, Creating and Connecting Observables, Observers, and Subjects*.

This illustrates a simplified way to turn Java's IO streams into `Observable` instances. Of course, with this main loop, the main thread of the program will block waiting for user input. This can be prevented using the right `Scheduler` instances to move the logic to another thread. We'll revisit this topic in *Chapter 6, Using Concurrency and Parallelism with Schedulers*.

Now, every line the user types into the terminal is propagated as a notification by the `ConnectableObservable` instance created by this method. The time has come to look at how we connect our value `Observable` instances, representing the collectors of the sum, to this input `Observable` instance. Here is the implementation of the `varStream(String, Observable)` method, which takes a name of a value and source `Observable` instance and returns an `Observable` instance representing this value:

```
public static Observable<Double> varStream(final String varName,
Observable<String> input) {
  final Pattern pattern = Pattern.compile("\\^s*" + varName +
  "\\s*[:|=]\\s*(-?\\d+\\.?\\d*)$"); // (1)
  return input
  .map(new Func1<String, Matcher>() {
    public Matcher call(String str) {
      return pattern.matcher(str); // (2)
    }
  })
  .filter(new Func1<Matcher, Boolean>() {
    public Boolean call(Matcher matcher) {
      return matcher.matches() && matcher.group(1) != null; //
      (3)
    }
  })
  .map(new Func1<Matcher, Double>() {
    public Double call(Matcher matcher) {
      return Double.parseDouble(matcher.group(1)); // (4)
```

```
      }
    });
  }
```

The `map()` and `filter()` methods called on the `Observable` instance here are part of the fluent API provided by RxJava. They can be called on an `Observable` instance, creating a new `Observable` instance that depends on these methods and that transforms or filters the incoming data. Using these methods the right way, you can express complex logic in a series of steps leading to your objective. Read more about this in *Chapter 4, Transforming, Filtering, and Accumulating Your Data*. Let's analyze the code:

1. Our variables are interested only in messages in the format `<var_name>: <value>` or `<var_name> = <value>`, so we are going to use this regular expression to filter and process only these kinds of messages. Remember that our input `Observable` instance sends each line the user writes; it is our job to handle it the right way.

2. Using the messages we receive from the input, we create a `Matcher` instance using the preceding regular expression as a pattern.

3. We pass through only data that matches the regular expression. Everything else is discarded.

4. Here, the value to set is extracted as a `Double` number value.

This is how the values a and b are represented by streams of double values, changing in time. Now we can implement their sum. We implemented it as a class that implements the `Observer` interface, because I wanted to show you another way of subscribing to `Observable` instances—using the `Observer` interface. Here is the code:

```
public static final class ReactiveSum implements Observer<Double>
{ // (1)
  private double sum;
  public ReactiveSum(Observable<Double> a, Observable<Double> b) {
    this.sum = 0;
    Observable.combineLatest(a, b, new Func2<Double, Double,
    Double>() { // (5)
      public Double call(Double a, Double b) {
        return a + b;
      }
    }).subscribe(this); // (6)
  }
  public void onCompleted() {
    System.out.println("Exiting last sum was : " + this.sum); //
    (4)
```

```
    }
    public void onError(Throwable e) {
      System.err.println("Got an error!"); // (3)
      e.printStackTrace();
    }
    public void onNext(Double sum) {
      this.sum = sum;
      System.out.println("update : a + b = " + sum); // (2)
    }
  }
}
```

This is the implementation of the actual sum, dependent on the two `Observable` instances representing its collectors:

1. It is an `Observer` interface. The `Observer` instance can be passed to the `Observable` instance's `subscribe(Observer)` method and defines three methods that are named after the three types of notification: `onNext(T)`, `onError(Throwable)`, and `onCompleted`. Read more about this interface in *Chapter 3, Creating and Connecting Observables, Observers, and Subjects.*

2. In our `onNext(Double)` method implementation, we set the sum to the incoming value and print an update to the standard output.

3. If we get an error, we just print it.

4. When everything is done, we greet the user with the final sum.

5. We implement the sum with the `combineLatest(Observable, Observable, Func2)` method. This method creates a new `Observable` instance. The new `Observable` instance is updated when any of the two `Observable` instances, passed to combineLatest receives an update. The value emitted through the new `Observable` instance is computed by the third parameter – a function that has access to the latest values of the two source sequences. In our case, we sum up the values. There will be no notification until both of the `Observable` instances passed to the method emit at least one value. So, we will have the sum only when both a and b have notifications. Read more about this method and other combiners in *Chapter 5, Combinators, Conditionals, and Error Handling.*

6. We subscribe our `Observer` instance to the combined `Observable` instance.

Here is sample of what the output of this example would look like:

```
Reacitve Sum. Type 'a: <number>' and 'b: <number>' to try it.
a:4
b:5
update : a + b = 9.0
```

```
a:6
update : a + b = 11.0
```

So this is it! We have implemented our reactive sum using streams of data.

 The source code of this example can be downloaded and tried out from here: `https://github.com/meddle0x53/learning-rxjava/blob/master/src/main/java/com/packtpub/reactive/chapter01/ReactiveSumV1.java`.

Summary

In this chapter, we went through the reactive principles and the reasons we should learn and use them. It is not so hard to build a reactive application; it just requires structuring the program in little declarative steps. With RxJava, this can be accomplished by building multiple asynchronous streams connected the right way, transforming the data all the way through its consumer.

The two examples presented in this chapter may look a bit complex and confusing at first glance, but in reality, they are pretty simple. There are a lot of new things in them, but everything will be explained in detail in the following chapters.

If you want to read more about reactive programming, take a look at *Reactive Programming in the Netflix API with RxJava*, a fine article on the topic, available at `http://techblog.netflix.com/2013/02/rxjava-netflix-api.html`. Another fine post introducing the concept can be found here: `https://gist.github.com/staltz/868e7e9bc2a7b8c1f754`.

And these are slides about reactive programming and RX by Ben Christensen, one of the creators of RxJava: `https://speakerdeck.com/benjchristensen/reactive-programming-with-rx-at-qconsf-2014`.

In the next chapter, we are going to talk about some of the concepts of *functional programming* and their implementation in Java 8. This will give us the basic ideas needed in the rest of the chapters and will help us get rid of Java verbosity when writing reactive programs.

2
Using the Functional Constructions of Java 8

Functional programming is not a new idea; actually, it's pretty old. For example, **Lisp**, which is a functional language, is the second oldest of today's commonly-used programming languages.

Functional programs are built using small pieces of reusable pure functions (lambdas). The program logic is composed of small declarative steps and not complex algorithms. That's because functional programs minimize the use of state, which makes imperative programs complex and hard to refactor/support.

With Java 8, the Java world got the lambda expressions and the ability to pass functions to functions. With them, we can code in a more functional style and get rid of a lot of the boilerplate code. The other new thing we got with Java 8 is the streams—something very similar to RxJava's observables but not asynchronous. Combining these streams and the lambdas, we are able to create more functional-like programs.

We are going to familiarize ourselves with these new constructions and look at how they can be used with RxJava's abstractions. Our programs will be simpler and easier to follow by using the lambdas, and the concepts introduced in this chapter will be of help while designing applications.

This chapter covers:

- Lambdas in Java 8
- First RxJava examples using the lambda syntax
- What pure functions and higher order functions are

Lambdas in Java 8

The most important change in Java 8 is the introduction of lambda expressions. They enable faster, clearer coding and make it possible to use functional programming.

Java was created back in the '90s as an object-oriented programming language, with the idea that everything should be an object. At that time, object-oriented programming was the principal paradigm for software development. But, recently, functional programming has become increasingly popular because it is well-suited for concurrent and event-driven programming. This doesn't mean that we should stop writing code using object-oriented languages. Instead, the best strategy is to mix elements of object-oriented and functional programming. Adding lambdas to Java 8 ties in with this idea – Java is an object-oriented language, but now it has lambdas, we are able to code using the functional style too.

Let's look at this new feature in detail.

Introducing the new syntax and semantics

In order to introduce lambda expressions, we need to see their actual value. This is why this chapter will begin with one example implemented without using lambda expressions, followed by re-implementing the same example using lambda expressions.

Remember the `map(Func1)` method from the `Observable` class? Let's try to implement something similar for the `java.util.List` collections. Of course, Java doesn't support adding methods to existing classes, so the implementation will be a static method that takes a list and transformation and returns a new list containing the transformed elements. In order to pass a transformation to the method, we'll need an interface with one method representing it.

Let's look at the code:

```
interface Mapper<V, M> { // (1)
  M map(V value); // (2)
}

// (3)
public static <V, M> List<M> map(List<V> list, Mapper<V, M>
mapper) {
  List<M> mapped = new ArrayList<M>(list.size()); // (4)
  for (V v : list) {
    mapped.add(mapper.map(v)); // (5)
  }
```

```
    return mapped; // (6)
  }
```

What is happening here?

1. We define a generic interface, called `Mapper`.

2. It has only one method, `M map(V)`, that receives a value of type `V` and transforms it to a value of type `M`.

3. The static method `List<M> map(List<V>, Mapper<V, M>)` takes one list with elements of type `V` and a `Mapper` implementation. Using this `Mapper` implementation's `map()` method on every element of the source list, it converts the list to a new list of type `M` containing the transformed elements.

4. The implementation creates a new empty list of type `M` with the same size as the source list.

5. Every element in the source list is transformed using the passed `Mapper` implementation and added to the new list.

6. The new list is returned.

In this implementation, every time we want to create a new list by transforming another, we will have to implement the `Mapper` interface with the right transformation. Until Java 8, the right way of passing custom logic to methods was exactly like this — with anonymous class instances, implementing the given methods.

But let's look at how we use this `List<M> map(List<V>, Mapper<V, M>)` method:

```
List<Integer> mapped = map(numbers, new Mapper<Integer, Integer>()
{
  @Override
  public Integer map(Integer value) {
    return value * value; // actual mapping
  }
});
```

In order to apply a mapping to a list, we need to write four lines of boilerplate code. The actual mapping is very simple and is only one of these lines. The real problem here is that instead of passing an action, we are passing an object. This obscures the real intention of this program — to pass an action that produces transformation from every item of the source list and to get a list with applied changes at the end.

Here is what this call looks like using the new lambda syntax of Java 8:

```
List<Integer> mapped = map(numbers, value -> value * value);
```

Pretty straight forward, isn't it? And it just works. Instead of passing an object and implementing an interface, we pass a block of code, a nameless function.

What is going on? We defined an arbitrary interface with an arbitrary method, but we could pass this lambda in place of an instance of the interface. In Java 8, if you define *interface with only one abstract method* and you create a method that receives a parameter of this type of interface, you can pass a lambda instead. If the interface single method takes two arguments of type string and returns an integer value, the lambda will have to be composed of two arguments before the ` -> ` and to return integer, the arguments will be inferred as strings.

Interfaces of this type are called **functional interfaces.** It is important for the single method to be abstract and not default. Another new thing in Java 8 is the default methods of interfaces:

```
interface Program {
  default String fromChapter() {
    return "Two";
  }
}
```

The default methods are useful when changing already existing interfaces. When we add default methods to them, the classes implementing them won't break. An interface with only one default method is not functional; a single method shouldn't be default.

Lambdas act as implementations of the functional interfaces. So, it is possible to assign them to variables of type interface as follows:

```
Mapper<Integer, Integer> square = (value) -> value * value;
```

And we can reuse the square object as it's an implementation of the `Mapper` interface.

Maybe you've noticed, but in the examples up until now, the parameters of lambda expressions have no type. That is because the types are inferred. So this expression is absolutely the same as the preceding expression:

```
Mapper<Integer, Integer> square = (Integer value) -> value * value;
```

The fact that the example with a parameter without a type works is not magic. Java is a statically typed language, so the parameter of the single method of the functional interface is used for type checking.

How about the body of the lambda expression? There is no `return` statement anywhere. It turns out that these two examples are exactly the same:

```
Mapper<Integer, Integer> square = (value) -> value * value;

// and
Mapper<Integer, Integer> square = (value) -> {

  return value * value;
};
```

The first expression is just a short form of the second. It is preferred for the lambda to be only one line of code. But if the lambda expression contains more than one line, the only way to define it is using the second approach, like this:

```
Mapper<Integer, Integer> square = (value) -> {
  System.out.println("Calculating the square of " + value);
  return value * value;
};
```

Under the hood, lambda expressions are not just syntax sugar for anonymous inner classes. They are implemented to perform quickly inside the **Java Virtual Machine (JVM)**, so if your code is designed to be compatible only with Java 8+, you should definitely use them. Their main idea is to pass around behavior in the same way that data is passed. This makes your program more human readable.

One last thing related to the new syntax is the ability to pass to methods and assign to variables already defined functions and methods. Let's define a new functional interface:

```
interface Action<V> {
  void act(V value);
}
```

We can use it to execute arbitrary actions for each value in a list; for example, logging the list. Here is a method that uses this interface:

```
public static <V> void act(List<V> list, Action<V> action) {
  for (V v : list) {
    action.act(v);
  }
}
```

This method is similar to the `map()` function. It iterates through the list and calls the passed action's `act()` method on every element. Let's call it using a lambda that simply logs the elements in the list:

```
act(list, value -> System.out.println(value));
```

This is quite simple but not necessary because the `println()` method can be passed itself to the `act()` method. This is done as follows:

```
act(list, System.out::println);
```

 The code for these examples can be viewed/downloaded at
https://github.com/meddle0x53/learning-rxjava/
blob/master/src/main/java/com/packtpub/reactive/
chapter02/Java8LambdasSyntaxIntroduction.java.

This is valid syntax in Java 8—every method can become a lambda and can be assigned to a variable or passed to a method. All these are valid:

- Book::makeBook // Static method of a class
- book::read // method of an instance
- Book::new // Constructor of a class
- Book::read // instance method, but referenced without using an actual instance.

Now that we've revealed the lambda syntax, we will be using it in our RxJava examples instead of anonymous inner classes.

Functional interfaces in Java 8 and RxJava

Java 8 comes with a special package containing functional interfaces for common cases. This package is `java.util.function`, and we are not going to look at it in detail in this book, but will present some of them that are worth mentioning:

- `Consumer<T>`: This represents a function that accepts an argument and returns nothing. Its abstract method is `void accept(T)`. As an example, we can use it to assign the `System.out::println` method to a variable, as follows:

```
Consumer<String> print = System.out::println;
```

- `Function<T,R>`: This represents a function that accepts one argument of a given type and returns a result of an arbitrary type. Its abstract method is `R accept(T)`, and it can be used for mapping. We don't need the `Mapper` interface at all! Let's take a look at the following code snippet:

```
Function<Integer, String> toStr = (value) -> (value + "!");
List<String> string = map(integers, toStr);
```

- `Predicate<T>`: This stands for a function with only one argument that returns a Boolean result. Its abstract method is `boolean test(T)` and it can be used for filtering. Let's take a look at the following code:

```
Predicate<Integer> odd = (value) -> value % 2 != 0;
```

There are a lot of functional interfaces similar to these; for example, a function with two arguments, or a binary operator. This is again a function with two arguments, but both of the same type and returning a result with the same type. They are there to help reuse lambdas in our code.

The good thing is that RxJava is lambda compatible. This means that the actions we were passing to the `subscribe` method are in fact functional interfaces!

RxJava's functional interfaces are in the `rx.functions` package. All of them extend a base **marker interface** (interface with no methods, used for type checking), called `Function`. Additionally, there is another marker interface, extending the `Function` one, called `Action`. It is used to mark consumers (functions, returning nothing).

RxJava has eleven `Action` interfaces:

```
Action0 // Action with no parameters
Action1<T1> // Action with one parameter
Action2<T1,T2> // Action with two parameters
Action9<T1,T2,T3,T4,T5,T6,T7,T8,T9> // Action with nine parameters
ActionN // Action with arbitrary number of parameters
```

They can be used mainly for subscriptions (`Action1` and `Action0`). The `Observable.OnSubscribe<T>` parameter, which we saw in *Chapter 1, An Introduction to Reactive Programming*, (used for creating custom observables) extends the `Action` interface too.

Analogically, there are eleven `Function` extenders representing function returning result. They are `Func0<R>`, `Func1<T1, R>` ... `Func9<T1,T2,T3,T4,T5,T6,T7,T8,T9 ,R>`, and `FuncN<R>`. They are used for mapping, filtering, combining, and many other purposes.

Every operator and subscribe method in RxJava is applicable to one or more of these interfaces. This means that we can use lambda expressions instead of anonymous inner classes in RxJava almost everywhere. From this point on, all our examples will use lambdas in order to be more readable and somewhat functional.

Now, let's look at one big RxJava example implemented with lambdas. This is our familiar Reactive Sum example!

Implementing the reactive sum example with lambdas

So this time, our main piece of code will be quite similar to the previous one:

```
ConnectableObservable<String> input =
CreateObservable.from(System.in);

Observable<Double> a = varStream("a", input);
Observable<Double> b = varStream("b", input);

reactiveSum(a, b); // The difference

input.connect();
```

The only difference is that we are going to take a more functional approach in calculating our sum and not to keep the same state. We won't be implementing the `Observer` interface; instead, we are going to pass lambdas to subscribe. This solution is much cleaner.

The `CreateObservable.from(InputStream)` method is a lot like we used previously. We will skip it and look at the `Observable<Double>` `varStream(String, Observable<String>)` method, which creates the `Observable` instances representing the collectors:

```
public static Observable<Double> varStream(
  final String name, Observable<String> input) {
    final Pattern pattern =      Pattern.compile(
      "\\s*" + name + "\\s*[:|=]\\s*(-?\\d+\\.?\\d*)$"
    );
    return input
    .map(pattern::matcher) // (1)
    .filter(m -> m.matches() && m.group(1) != null) // (2)
    .map(matcher -> matcher.group(1)) // (3)
    .map(Double::parseDouble); // (4)
  }
)
```

This method is much shorter than used previously and looks simpler. But semantically, it is the same. It creates an `Observable` instance connected to a source observable producing arbitrary strings, and if a string is in the format it expects, it extracts a double number from it and emits this number. The logic responsible for checking the format of the input and extracting the number is only four lines and is represented by simple lambdas. Let's examine it:

1. We map a lambda that creates a `matcher` instance using the pattern expected and the input string.

2. Using the `filter()` method, only the input that is in the right format is filtered.

3. Using a `map()` operator, we create a string from the `matcher` instance, which contains only the number data we need.

4. And again with the `map()` operator, the string is turned into a double number.

And as for the new `void reactiveSum(Observable<Double>, Observable<Double>)` method's implementation, use the following code:

```
public static void reactiveSum(
   Observable<Double> a,
   Observable<Double> b) {
   Observable
      .combineLatest(a, b, (x, y) -> x + y) // (1)
      .subscribe( // (2)
         sum -> System.out.println("update : a + b = " + sum),
      error -> {
      System.out.println("Got an error!");
      error.printStackTrace();
      },
      () -> System.out.println("Exiting...")
   );
}
```

Let's take a look at the following code:

1. Again, we use the `combineLatest()` method, but this time the third argument is a simple lambda that implements a sum.

2. The `subscribe()` method takes three lambda expressions that are triggered when the following events occur:

   ° The sum changes

   ° There is an error

   ° The program is about to finish

The source of this example can be viewed/downloaded at `https://github.com/meddle0x53/learning-rxjava/blob/master/src/main/java/com/packtpub/reactive/chapter02/ReactiveSumV2.java`.

Everything becomes simpler using lambdas. Looking at the preceding program, we can see that most of the logic is composed of small, independent functions, chained using other functions. This is what we mean by being functional, to express our programs using such small reusable functions that take other functions and return functions and data abstractions, which transform input data using chains of functions in order to produce the wanted result. But let's look at these functions in depth.

Pure functions and higher order functions

You don't have to remember most of the terms introduced in this chapter; the important thing is to understand how they help us write simplistic but powerful programs.

RxJava's approach has many functional ideas incorporated, so it is important for us to learn how to think in more functional ways in order to write better reactive applications.

Pure functions

A **pure function** is a function whose return value is only determined by its input, without observable **side effects**. If we call it with the same parameters n times, we are going to get the same result every single time. For example:

```
Predicate<Integer> even = (number) -> number % 2 == 0;
int i = 50;
while((i--) > 0) {
   System.out.println("Is five even? - " + even.test(5));
}
```

Each time, the even function returns `False` because it *depends only on its input*, which is the same each time and is not even.

This property of pure functions is called **idempotence**. Idempotent functions don't depend on time, so they can treat continuous data as infinite data streams. And this is how ever-changing data is represented in RxJava (`Observable` instances).

 Note that, here, the term "idempotence" is used in its computer science meaning. In computing, an idempotent operation is one that has no additional effect if it is called more than once with the same input parameters; in mathematics, an idempotent operation is one that satisfies this expression: $f(f(x)) = f(x)$.

Pure functions *do not cause side-effects*. For example:

```
Predicate<Integer> impureEven = (number) -> {
  System.out.println("Printing here is side effect!");
  return number % 2 == 0;
};
```

This function is not pure because it prints on the output a message every time it is called. So it does two things: it tests whether the number is even, and it outputs a message as a side-effect. A side-effect is any possible observable output the function can produce, for example, triggering events and throwing exceptions and I/O, different from its return value. A side-effect also changes shared states or mutable arguments.

Think about it. If most of your program is composed of pure functions, it will be easy to scale and to run parts of it in parallel because pure functions can't conflict with each other and don't change the shared state.

Another thing that's worth mentioning in this section is **immutability**. Immutable objects are objects that can not change their state. A good example is the `String` class in Java. The `String` instances cannot be changed; even methods such as `substring` create a new instance of `String` without modifying the calling one.

If we pass immutable data to a pure function, we can be sure that every time it is called with this data it will return the same. With **mutable** objects, is not quite the same when we write parallel programs, because one thread can change the object's state. In this case, the pure function will return a different result if called, and thus will stop being idempotent.

If we store our data in immutable objects and operate over it using pure functions, creating new immutable objects in the process, we will be safe from unexpected concurrency issues. There will be no global state and no mutable state; everything will be simple and predictable.

Using immutable objects is tricky; every action with them creates new instances, and this could eat up memory. But there are methods for avoiding that; for example, reusing as much as we can from the source immutable, or making the immutable objects' lifecycles as short as possible (because short lifecycle objects are friendly to GC or caching). Functional programs should be designed to work with immutable stateless data.

Complex programs can't be composed only of pure functions, but whenever it is possible, it is good to use them. In this chapter's implementation of *The Reactive Sum*, we passed to `map()`, `filter()`, and `combineLatest()` only pure functions.

Speaking of the `map()` and `filter()` functions, we call them higher order functions.

Higher order functions

A function with at least one parameter of type function or a function that returns functions is called a **higher order function**. Of course, *higher order functions can be pure*.

Here is an example of a higher function that takes function parameters:

```java
public static <T, R> int highSum(
   Function<T, Integer> f1,
   Function<R, Integer> f2,
   T data1,
   R data2) {
     return f1.apply(data1) + f2.apply(data2);
   }
)
```

It takes two functions of type `T -> int`/`R -> int` and some data in order to call them and sum their results. For example, we can do it like this:

```java
highSum(v -> v * v, v -> v * v * v, 3, 2);
```

Here we sum the square of three and the cube of two.

But the idea of higher order functions is to be flexible. For example, we can use the `highSum()` function for a completely different purpose, say, summing strings, as shown here:

```java
Function<String, Integer> strToInt = s -> Integer.parseInt(s);

highSum(strToInt, strToInt, "4",  "5");
```

So, a higher order function can be used to apply the same behavior to different kinds of input.

If the first two arguments we pass to the `highSum()` function are pure functions, it will be a pure function as well. The `strToInt` parameter is a pure function, and if we call the `highSum(strToInt, strToInt, "4", "5")` method *n* times, it will return the same result and won't have side-effects.

Here is another example of a higher order function:

```
public static Function<String, String> greet(String greeting) {
    return (String name) -> greeting + " " + name + "!";
}
```

This is a function that returns another function. It can be used like this:

```
System.out.println(greet("Hello").apply("world"));
// Prints 'Hellow world!'

System.out.println(greet("Goodbye").apply("cruel world"));
// Prints 'Goodbye cruel world!'

Function<String, String> howdy = greet("Howdy");

System.out.println(howdy.apply("Tanya"));
System.out.println(howdy.apply("Dali"));
// These two print 'Howdy Tanya!' and 'Howdy Dali'
```

 The code for this example can be found at `https://github.com/meddle0x53/learning-rxjava/blob/master/src/main/java/com/packtpub/reactive/chapter02/PureAndHigherOrderFunctions.java`.

Functions like these can be used to implement different behaviors that have something in common. In object-oriented programming we define classes and then extend them, overloading their methods. In functional programming, we define higher order functions as interfaces and call them with different parameters, resulting in different behaviors.

These functions are *first-class citizens*; we can code our logic using only functions, chaining them, and handling our data, transforming, filtering, or accumulating it into a result.

RxJava and functional programming

Functional concepts such as pure functions and higher order functions are very important to RxJava. RxJava's `Observable` class is an implementation of a *fluent interface*. This means that most of its instance methods return an `Observable` instance. For example:

```
Observable mapped = observable.map(someFunction);
```

The `map()` operator returns a new `Observable` instance, emitting the data transformed by it. Operators such as `map()` are clearly higher order functions, and we can pass other functions to them. So, a typical RxJava program is represented by a chain of operators chained to an `Observable` instance to which multiple *subscribers* can subscribe. These functions chained together can benefit from the topics covered in this chapter. We can pass lambdas to them instead of anonymous interface implementations (as we saw with the second implementation of the *Reactive Sum*), and we should try working with immutable data and pure functions when possible. This way, our code will be simple and safe.

Summary

In this chapter, we've looked at some of the functional programming principles and terms. We've learned how to write programs composed of small pure function actions, chained together using higher order functions.

As functional programming is getting increasingly popular, developers proficient in it will be in high demand in the very near future. That's because it helps us achieve scalability and parallelism with ease. And what is more, if we add the reactive idea to it, it becomes even more appealing.

That's why we are going to dive into the RxJava framework in the next chapters, learning how to use it for our benefit. We'll begin with the `Observable` instance creation techniques. This will provide us with the skill to create an `Observable` instance from everything, thus turning almost everything into a functional reactive program.

3
Creating and Connecting Observables, Observers, and Subjects

RxJava's `Observable` instances are the building blocks of reactive applications, and this advantage of RxJava is beneficial. If we have a source `Observable` instance, we could chain logic to it and *subscribe* for the result. All we need is this initial `Observable` instance.

In the browser or in a desktop application, user input is already represented by events that we can handle and forward through `Observable` instances. But it would be great to turn all of our data changes or actions into `Observable` instances, not just user input. For example, when we read data from a file, it would be neat to look at every line read or every sequence of bytes as a message that can be emitted through an `Observable` instance.

We'll look in detail at how different data sources can be transformed into `Observable` instances; it doesn't matter if they are external (files or user input) or internal (collections or scalars). What's more, we'll learn about the various types of `Observable` instances, depending on their behavior. Another important thing that we'll learn is how and when to unsubscribe from `Observable` instances and how to use subscriptions and `Observer` instances. Additionally, we'll present Subject type and its usage.

In this chapter, we will learn about:

- `Observable` factory methods — `just`, `from`, `create`, and others
- Observers and subscribers
- Hot and cold observables; connectable observables

- What subjects are and when to use them
- `Observable` creation

There are a lot of ways to create `Observable` instances from different sources. In principle, an `Observable` instance could be created using the `Observable.create(OnSubscribe<T>)` method, but there are many simple methods, implemented with the idea of making our life better. Let's look at some of them.

The Observable.from method

The `Observable.from` method can create an `Observable` instance from different Java structures. For example:

```
List<String> list = Arrays.asList(
   "blue", "red", "green", "yellow", "orange", "cyan", "purple"
);
Observable<String> listObservable = Observable.from(list);
listObservable.subscribe(System.out::println);
```

This piece of code creates an `Observable` instance from a `List` instance. When the `subscribe` method is called on the `Observable` instance, all of the elements contained in the source list are emitted to the subscribing method. For every call to the `subscribe()` method, the whole collection is emitted from the beginning, element by element:

```
listObservable.subscribe(
   color -> System.out.print(color + "|"),
   System.out::println,
   System.out::println
);
listObservable.subscribe(color -> System.out.print(color + "/"));
```

This will print the colors twice with different formatting.

The true signature of this version of the `from` method is `final static <T> Observable<T> from(Iterable<? extends T> iterable)`. This means that an instance from any class, implementing the `Iterable` interface can be passed to this method. These include any Java collection, for example:

```
Path resources = Paths.get("src", "main", "resources");
try (DirectoryStream<Path> dStream
=Files.newDirectoryStream(resources)) {
   Observable<Path> dirObservable = Observable.from(dStream);
   dirObservable.subscribe(System.out::println);
}
```

```
catch (IOException e) {
  e.printStackTrace();
}
```

This turns the contents of a folder to events to which we can subscribe. That's possible because the `DirectoryStream` parameter is an `Iterable` instance. Note that on every call to the `subscribe` method of this `Observable` instance, its `Iterable` source's `iterator()` method is called to obtain a new `Iterator` instance to be used to traverse the data from the beginning. With this example, a `java.lang.IllegalStateException` exception will be thrown on the second call to the `subscribe()` method, because the `iterator()` method of the `DirectoryStream` parameter can be called only once.

Another overload of the `from` method used to create `Observable` instances from arrays is `public final static <T> Observable<T> from(T[] array)`, and an example of using `Observable` instances is as follows:

```
Observable<Integer> arrayObservable =
  Observable.from(new Integer[] {3, 5, 8});
  arrayObservable.subscribe(System.out::println);
```

The `Observable.from()` method is very useful for creating the `Observable` instances from collections or arrays. But there are cases when we need to create the `Observable` instance from a single object; for these, the `Observable.just()` method can be used.

 The source code for the examples of using the `Observable.from()` method can be viewed and downloaded at https://github.com/meddle0x53/learning-rxjava/blob/master/src/main/java/com/packtpub/reactive/chapter03/CreatingObservablesWithFrom.java.

The Observable.just method

The `just()` method emits its parameter(s) as `OnNext` notifications, and after that, it emits an `OnCompleted` notification.

For example, one letter:

```
Observable.just('S').subscribe(System.out::println);
```

Or a sequence of letters:

```
Observable
  .just('R', 'x', 'J', 'a', 'v', 'a')
  .subscribe(
```

```
        System.out::print,
        System.err::println,
        System.out::println
    );
```

The first piece of code prints `s` and a new line, and the second prints the letters on a single line and adds a new line on completion. The method allows up to nine arbitrary values (objects of the same type) to be observed through reactive means. For example, say we have this simple `User` class:

```
public static class User {
    private final String forename;
    private final String lastname;
    public User(String forename, String lastname) {
        this.forename = forename;
        this.lastname = lastname;
    }
    public String getForename() {
        return this.forename;
    }
    public String getLastname() {
        return this.lastname;
    }
}
```

We can print the full name of a `User` instance like this:

```
Observable
    .just(new User("Dali", "Bali"))
    .map(u -> u.getForename() + " " + u.getLastname())
    .subscribe(System.out::println);
```

This is not very practical but showcases putting data in the `Observable` instance context and taking advantage of the `map()` method. Everything can become an event.

There are a few more convenient factory methods, usable in all kinds of situations. Let's take a look at them in the next section.

 The source code of the example of the `Observable.just()` method can be viewed/downloaded at `https://github.com/meddle0x53/learning-rxjava/blob/master/src/main/java/com/packtpub/reactive/chapter03/CreatingObservablesUsingJust.java`.

Other Observable factory methods

Here, we will inspect a few methods that can be used in combination with transforming operators such as flatMap or combining operators such as .zip file (more about this in the next chapter).

In order to examine their results, we will use the following method for creating subscriptions:

```
void subscribePrint(Observable<T> observable, String name) {
  observable.subscribe(
    (v) -> System.out.println(name + " : " + v),
    (e) -> {
      System.err.println("Error from " + name + ":");
      System.err.println(e.getMessage());
    },
    () -> System.out.println(name + " ended!")
  );
}
```

The idea of the preceding method is to *subscribe* to an Observable instance and label it with a name. On *OnNext*, it prints the value prefixed with the name; on *OnError*, it prints the error together with the name; and on *OnCompleted*, it prints 'ended!' prefixed with the name. This helps us debug the results.

 The source code of the preceding method can be found at https://github.com/meddle0x53/learning-rxjava/blob/4a2598aa0835235e6ef3bc3371a3c19896161628/src/main/java/com/packtpub/reactive/common/Helpers.java#L25.

Here is the code introducing the new factory methods:

```
subscribePrint(
  Observable.interval(500L, TimeUnit.MILLISECONDS),
  "Interval Observable"
);
subscribePrint(
  Observable.timer(0L, 1L, TimeUnit.SECONDS),
  "Timed Interval Observable"
);
subscribePrint(
  Observable.timer(1L, TimeUnit.SECONDS),
  "Timer Observable"
);
```

```
subscribePrint(
  Observable.error(new Exception("Test Error!")),
  "Error Observable"
);
subscribePrint(Observable.empty(), "Empty Observable");
subscribePrint(Observable.never(), "Never Observable");
subscribePrint(Observable.range(1, 3), "Range Observable");
Thread.sleep(2000L);
```

Here's what's happening in the code:

- `Observable<Long> Observable.interval(long, TimeUnit, [Scheduler])`: This method creates an `Observable` instance that will emit sequential numbers at given intervals. It can be used to implement periodic polling, or continuous status logging, by just ignoring the number emitted and emitting useful messages. What's special about this method is that it's running on a *computation thread* by default. We can change that by passing a third argument to the method—a `Scheduler` instance (more about `Scheduler` instances in *Chapter 6, Using Concurrency and Parallelism with Schedulers*).

- `Observable<Long> Observable.timer(long, long, TimeUnit, [Scheduler])`: The `interval()` method begins emitting numbers only after it has waited for the specified time interval to pass. What if we want to tell it at what time exactly to begin working? We can do this using this `timer()` method. Its first argument is the starting time, and the second and the third are for interval setup. Again, it is executed on the *computation thread* by default, and again, this is configurable.

- `Observable<Long> Observable.timer(long, TimeUnit, [Scheduler])`: This one just emits the output `'0'` after a given amount of time on the *computation thread* (by default). After that, it emits a *completed* notification.

- `<T> Observable<T> Observable.error(Throwable)`: This emits just the error passed to it as an *OnError* notification. This is similar to the `'throw'` keyword in the classical, imperative Java world.

- `<T> Observable<T> Observable.empty()`: This one emits no items, but it emits a `OnCompleted` notification immediately.

- `<T> Observable<T> Observable.never()`: This does nothing. It sends no notifications to its `Observer` instances, and even the `OnCompleted` notification is not sent.

- `Observable<Integer> Observable.range(int, int, [Scheduler])`: This method sends sequential numbers beginning with the first parameter passed. The second parameter is the number of the emissions.

This program will print the following output:

```
Timed Interval Observable : 0
Error from Error Observable:
Test Error!
Range Observable : 1
Range Observable : 2
Range Observable : 3
Range Observable ended!
Empty Observable ended!
Interval Observable : 0
Interval Observable : 1
Timed Interval Observable : 1
Timer Observable : 0
Timer Observable ended!
Interval Observable : 2
Interval Observable : 3
Timed Interval Observable : 2
```

As you can see, the `interval Observable` instance doesn't send the *OnCompleted* notification. The program ends after two seconds and the `interval Observable` instance begins emitting after 500 milliseconds, every 500 milliseconds; thus, it emits three *OnNext* notifications. The `timed interval Observable` instance begins emitting immediately after its creation and emits every second; thus, we've got two notifications from it.

> The source code of the preceding example can be viewed/downloaded at https://github.com/meddle0x53/learning-rxjava/blob/master/src/main/java/com/packtpub/reactive/chapter03/CreatingObservablesUsingVariousFactoryMethods.java.

All of these methods are implemented using the `Observable.create()` method.

The Observable.create method

Let's look at the signature of the method first:

```
public final static <T> Observable<T> create(OnSubscribe<T>)
```

It takes a parameter of type OnSubscribe. This interface extends the Action1<Subscriber<? super T>> interface; in other words, this type has only one method, taking one argument of type Subscriber<T> and returning nothing. This function will be called every time the Observable.subscribe() method is invoked. Its argument, an instance of the Subscriber class, is in fact the observer, subscribing to the Observable instance (here, the Subscriber class and Observer interface have the same role). We'll be talking about them later in this chapter). We can invoke the onNext(), onError(), and onCompleted() methods on it, implementing our own custom behavior.

It's easier to comprehend this with an example. Let's implement a simple version of the Observable.from(Iterabale<T>) method:

```
<T> Observable<T> fromIterable(final Iterable<T> iterable) {
  return Observable.create(new OnSubscribe<T>() {
    @Override
    public void call(Subscriber<? super T> subscriber) {
      try {
        Iterator<T> iterator = iterable.iterator(); // (1)
        while (iterator.hasNext()) { // (2)
          subscriber.onNext(iterator.next());
        }
        subscriber.onCompleted(); // (3)
      }
      catch (Exception e) {
        subscriber.onError(e); // (4)
      }
    }
  });
}
```

The method takes an Iterable<T> parameter as an argument and returns an Observable<T> parameter. The behavior is as follows:

1. When an Observer/Subscriber instance subscribes to the resulting Observable instance, an Iterator instance is retrieved from the Iterable source. The Subscriber class actually implements the Observer interface. It is an abstract class, and the on* methods are not implemented by it.

2. While there are elements, they are emitted as OnNext notifications.

3. And when all the elements are emitted, an OnCompleted notification is dispatched.

4. If at any time an error occurs, an OnError notification is dispatched with the error.

This is a very simple and naive implementation of the behavior of the `Observable`. `from(Iterable<T>)` method. The Reactive Sum described in the first and second chapters is another example of the power of the `Observable.create` method (used by `CreateObservable.from()`).

But as we saw, the logic passed to the `create()` method is triggered when the `Observable.subscribe()` method is invoked on the `Observable` instance. Until now, we were creating `Observable` instances and *subscribing* to them with this method. It is time to look at it in detail.

Subscribing and unsubscribing

The `Observable.subscribe()` method has many overloads as follows:

- `subscribe()`: This one ignores all the emissions from the `Observable` instance and throws an `OnErrorNotImplementedException` exception if there is an `OnError` notification. This can be used to only trigger the `OnSubscribe.call` behavior.

- `subscribe(Action1<? super T>)`: This only subscribes to `onNext()` method-triggered updates. It ignores the `OnCompleted` notification and throws an `OnErrorNotImplementedException` exception if there is an `OnError` notification. It is not a good choice for real production code, because it is hard to guarantee that no errors will be thrown.

- `subscribe(Action1<? super T>, Action1<Throwable>)`: This is the same as preceding one, but the second parameter is called if there is an `OnError` notification.

- `subscribe(Action1<? super T>,Action1<Throwable>, Action0)`: This is the same as the preceding one, but the third parameter is called on `OnCompleted` notification.

- `subscribe(Observer<? super T>)`: This uses its `Observer` parameter's `onNext/onError/onCompleted` methods to observe the notifications from the `Observable` instance. We used this in the first chapter while implementing "The Reactive Sum".

- `subscribe(Subscriber<? super T>)`: This is the same as the preceding one, but the `Subscriber` implementation of the `Observer` interface is used to observe notifications. The `Subscriber` class provides advanced functionality, such as unsubscription (cancellation) and backpressure (flow control). Actually, all the preceding methods call this one; that's why we will be referring to it when talking about `Observable.subscribe` from now on. The method ensures that the `Subscriber` instance passed sees an `Observable` instance, complying with the following **Rx contract**:

> *"Messages sent to instances of the Observer interface follow the following syntax:*
>
> *onNext* (onCompleted | onError)?*
>
> *This syntax allows observable sequences to send any number (0 or more) of* OnNext() *method messages to the Subscriber, optionally followed by a single success (onCompleted) or failure (onError) message. The single message indicating that an observable sequence has finished ensures that consumers of the observable sequence can deterministically establish that it is safe to perform cleanup operations. A single failure further ensures that abort semantics can be maintained for operators that work on multiple observable sequences".*

– part of RxJava's JavaDoc.

This is done internally by using a wrapper around the passed Subscriber instance — SafeSubscriber.

- unsafeSubscribe(Subscriber<? super T>): This is the same as the preceding one but without the **Rx contract** protection. It is meant to help implement custom operators (see *Chapter 8, Resource Management and Extending RxJava*) without the additional overhead of the subscribe() method's protections; using this method to observe an Observable instance in general code is discouraged.

All of these methods return results of type Subscription that can be used for *unsubscribing* from the notifications emitted by the Observable instance. Unsubscribing usually cleans up internal resources associated with a subscription; for example, if we implement an HTTP request with the Observable.create() method and want to cancel it by a particular time, or we have an Observable instance emitting a sequence of numbers/words/arbitrary data infinitely and want to stop that.

The Subscription interface has two methods:

- void unsubscribe(): This is used for *unsubscribing*.
- boolean isUnsubscribed(): This is used to check whether the Subscription instance is already *unsubscribed*.

The instance of the `Subscriber` class, passed to the `Observable.create()` method's `OnSubscribe()` method, implements the `Subscription` interface. So, while coding the behavior of the `Observable` instance, *unsubscribing* and checking whether `Subscriber` is subscribed can be done. Let's update our `Observable<T> fromIterable(Iterable<T>)` method implementation to react on *unsubscribing*:

```
<T> Observable<T> fromIterable(final Iterable<T> iterable) {
  return Observable.create(new OnSubscribe<T>() {
    @Override
    public void call(Subscriber<? super T> subscriber) {
      try {
        Iterator<T> iterator = iterable.iterator();
        while (iterator.hasNext()) {
          if (subscriber.isUnsubscribed()) {
            return;
          }
          subscriber.onNext(iterator.next());
        }
        if (!subscriber.isUnsubscribed()) {
          subscriber.onCompleted();
        }
      }
      catch (Exception e) {
        if (!subscriber.isUnsubscribed()) {
          subscriber.onError(e);
        }
      }
    }
  });
}
```

The new thing here is that the `Subscription.isUnsubscribed()` method is used to determine whether the data emission should be terminated. We check whether the `Subscriber` is already *unsubscribed* on every iteration, because it can *unsubscribe* at any time and we won't need to emit anything after that. After everything is emitted, if the Subscriber is already *unsubscribed*, the `onCompleted()` method is skipped. If there is an exception , it is only emitted as an `OnError` notification if the `Subscriber` instance is still *subscribed*.

Let's look at how *unsubscribing* works:

```
Path path = Paths.get("src", "main", "resources",
"lorem_big.txt"); // (1)
List<String> data = Files.readAllLines(path);
Observable<String> observable =
fromIterable(data).subscribeOn(Schedulers.computation()); // (2)
Subscription subscription = subscribePrint(observable, "File");//
(3)
System.out.println("Before unsubscribe!");
System.out.println("-------------------");
subscription.unsubscribe(); // (4)
System.out.println("-------------------");
System.out.println("After unsubscribe!");
```

Here's what's happening in this example:

1. The data source is a huge file because we need something that takes some time to be iterated.

2. All the subscriptions to the `Observable` instance will take place on another *thread* because we will want to *unsubscribe* on the main thread.

3. The `subscribePrint()` method defined in this chapter is used, but it is modified to return the `Subscription`.

4. The subscription is used to *unsubscribe* from the `Observable` instance, so the whole file won't be printed and there are markers showing when the *unsubscription* is executed.

The output will be something like this:

```
File : Donec facilisis sollicitudin est non molestie.

File : Integer nec magna ac ex rhoncus imperdiet.

Before unsubscribe!

-------------------

File : Nullam pharetra iaculis sem.

-------------------

After unsubscribe!
```

So most of the file's content is skipped. Note that it is possible for something to be emitted right after *unsubscribing*; for example, if the `Subscriber` instance *unsubscribes* right after the check for *unsubscribing* and the program is already executing the body of the `if` statement, checking whether the user is unsubscribed.

The source code of the preceding example can be downloaded/viewed at https://github.com/meddle0x53/learning-rxjava/blob/master/src/main/java/com/packtpub/reactive/chapter03/ObservableCreateExample.java.

Another thing to note is that the Subscriber instances have a void add(Subscription s) method. Every subscription passed to it will be automatically *unsubscribed* when the Subscriber is *unsubscribed*. This way, we can add additional actions to the Subscriber instance; for example, actions that should be executed at *unsubscribing* (similar to the try — finally construction in Java). This is how *unsubscribing* works. In *Chapter 8, Resource Management and Extending RxJava*, we'll be dealing with resource management. We'll learn how Observable instances can be attached to Subscriber instances through a Subscription wrapper, and how calling *unsubscribe* will release any allocated resources.

The next topic we'll be covering in this chapter is related to subscribing behavior. We will be talking about hot and cold Observable instances.

Hot and cold Observable instances

Looking at the previous examples implemented using the Observable.create(), Observable.just(), and Observable.from() methods, we can say that until someone subscribes to them, they are inactive and don't emit anything. However, each time someone subscribes, they start emitting their notifications. For example, if we subscribe three times to an Observable.from(Iterable) object, the Iterable instance will be iterated *three* times. The Observable instances behaving like that are called cold Observable instances.

All of the factory methods we've been using in this chapter return cold Observables. Cold Observables produce notifications on demand, and for every Subscriber, they produce *independent* notifications.

There are Observable instances which, when they start emitting notifications, it doesn't matter if there are subscriptions to them or not. They continue emitting them until completion. All the subscribers receive the same notifications, and by default, when a Subscriber *subscribes*, it doesn't receive the notifications emitted before that. These are hot Observable instances.

We can say that cold Observables generate notifications for each subscriber and hot Observables are always running, broadcasting notifications to all of their subscribers. Think of a hot Observable as a radio station. All of the listeners that are listening to it at this moment listen to the same song. A cold Observable is a music CD. Many people can buy it and listen to it independently.

As we mentioned, there are a lot of examples in this book that use cold Observables. What about hot Observable instances? If you remember when we implemented 'The Reactive Sum' in the first chapter, we had an `Observable` instance that was emitting every line the user had typed in the standard input stream. This one was hot, and we forked two `Observable` instances from it, one for the collector a and one for b. They received the same input lines and filtered only the ones they were interested in. This input `Observable` instance was implemented using a special type of `Observable`, called `ConnectableObservable`.

The ConnectableObservable class

These `Observable` instances are inactive until their `connect()` method is called. After that, they become hot Observables. The `ConnectableObservable` instance can be created from any `Observable` instance by calling its `publish()` method. In other words, the `publish()` method can turn any cold Observable into a hot one. Let's look at this example:

```
Observable<Long> interval = Observable.interval(100L,
TimeUnit.MILLISECONDS);
ConnectableObservable<Long> published = interval.publish();
Subscription sub1 = subscribePrint(published, "First");
Subscription sub2 = subscribePrint(published, "Second");
published.connect();
Subscription sub3 = null;
try {
  Thread.sleep(500L);
  sub3 = subscribePrint(published, "Third");
  Thread.sleep(500L);
}
catch (InterruptedException e) {}
sub1.unsubscribe();
sub2.unsubscribe();
sub3.unsubscribe();
```

Nothing will happen until the `connect()` method is called. After that, we'll see the same sequential numbers outputted twice—once for each Subscriber. The third Subscriber will join the other two, printing the numbers emitted after the first 500 milliseconds, but it won't print the numbers emitted before its subscription.

What if we want to receive *all the* notifications that have been emitted before our subscription and then to continue receiving the incoming ones? That can be accomplished by calling the `replay()` method instead of the `publish()` method. It creates a `ConnectableObservable` instance from the source `Observable` instance with this little twist: all the subscribers, whenever they subscribe, will receive *all the* notifications (the previous notifications will arrive in order and synchronously).

There is a way to activate an `Observable` instance to become hot without calling the `connect()` method. It can be activated *on the first subscription* to it and deactivated when every `Subscriber` instance *unsubscribes*. Such an `Observable` instance can be created from a `ConnectableObservable` instance by calling the `refCount()` method on it (the name of the method comes from 'reference count'; it counts the `Subscriber` instances subscribed to the `Observable` instance created by it). Here is the preceding example implemented using the `refCount()` method:

```
Observable<Long> refCount = interval.publish().refCount();
Subscription sub1 = subscribePrint(refCount, "First");
Subscription sub2 = subscribePrint(refCount, "Second");
try {
  Thread.sleep(300L);
}
catch (InterruptedException e) {}
sub1.unsubscribe();
sub2.unsubscribe();
Subscription sub3 = subscribePrint(refCount, "Third");
try {
  Thread.sleep(300L);
}
catch (InterruptedException e) { }
sub3.unsubscribe();
```

The `Observable` instance will be deactivated when `sub2` *unsubscribes*. If someone *subscribes* to it after that, it will begin emitting the sequence from the beginning. This is what's happening with `sub3`. There is a `share()` method, which is an alias for the `publish().refCount()` call.

> The source code of the preceding example can be viewed/downloaded at https://github.com/meddle0x53/learning-rxjava/blob/master/src/main/java/com/packtpub/reactive/chapter03/UsingConnectableObservables.java.

There is one other way to create a hot Observable: using a `Subject` instance. We will introduce them in the next and last section of this chapter.

The Subject instances

The Subject instances are both Observable instances and Observer instances. Like Observable instances, they can have multiple Observer instances, receiving the same notifications. That's why they can be used to turn cold Observable instances into hot ones. Like Observer instances, they give us access to their onNext(), onError(), or onCompleted() methods.

Let's look at an implementation of the preceding hot *interval* examples, using a Subject instance:

```
Observable<Long> interval = Observable.interval(100L,
TimeUnit.MILLISECONDS); // (1)
Subject<Long, Long> publishSubject = PublishSubject.create(); // (2)
interval.subscribe(publishSubject);
// (3)
Subscription sub1 = subscribePrint(publishSubject, "First");
Subscription sub2 = subscribePrint(publishSubject, "Second");
Subscription sub3 = null;
try {
  Thread.sleep(300L);
  publishSubject.onNext(555L); // (4)
  sub3 = subscribePrint(publishSubject, "Third"); // (5)
  Thread.sleep(500L);
}
catch (InterruptedException e) {}
sub1.unsubscribe(); // (6)
sub2.unsubscribe();
sub3.unsubscribe();
```

The example is slightly different now:

1. The interval Observable instance is created the same way as before.

2. Here, we create a PublishSubject instance—a Subject instance that emits to an Observer instance only those items that are emitted by the source Observable instance subsequent to the time of the subscription. This behavior is similar to that of the ConnectableObservable instance created by the publish() method. The new Subject instance is subscribed to the interval Observable instance , created by the interval factory method, which is possible because the Subject class implements the Observer interface. Also, note that the Subject signature has two generic types—one for the type of notifications the Subject instance will receive and another for the type of the notifications it will emit. The PublishSubject class has the same type for its input and output *notifications*.

Note that it is possible to create a `PublishSubject` instance without subscribing to a source `Observable` instance. It will emit only the notifications passed to its `onNext()` and `onError()` methods and will complete when calling its `onCompleted()` method.

3. We can subscribe to the `Subject` instance; it is an `Observable` instance after all.

4. We can emit a custom notification at any time. It will be *broadcast* to all the subscribers of the subject. We can even call the `onCompleted()` method and close the notification stream.

5. The third Subscriber will only receive notifications emitted after it subscribes.

6. When everything *unsubscribes*, the `Subject` instance will continue emitting.

> This example's source code can be viewed/downloaded at `https://github.com/meddle0x53/learning-rxjava/blob/master/src/main/java/com/packtpub/reactive/chapter03/SubjectsDemonstration.java`.

There are four types of subjects that come with RxJava:

- `PublishSubject`: This is the one we saw in the previous example, behaving like `ConnectableObservable`, created using the `publish()` method.

- `ReplaySubject`: This emits to any observer all of the items that were emitted by the source `Observable` instance, regardless of when the observer subscribes. So, it behaves like `ConnectableObservable`, created using the `replay()` method. The `ReplaySubject` class has many factory methods. The default one caches everything; keep this in mind, because it can eat up memory. There are **factory methods** for creating it with size-bound and/or time-bound buffers. As with the `PublishSubject` class, this one can be used without a source `Observable` instance. All of the notifications emitted using its `onNext()`, `onError()`, and `onCompleted()` methods will be emitted to every Subscriber, even if it is subscribed after invoking the `on*` methods.

- `BehaviorSubject`: When an observer subscribes to it, it emits the item most recently emitted by the source `Observable` instance (or a seed/default value if none have yet been emitted) and then continues to emit any other items emitted later by the source `Observable` instance. The `BehaviorSubject` class is almost like the `ReplaySubjects` class with a buffer size of one. The `BehaviorSubject` class can be used to implement a stateful reactive instance—a reactive property. Again, a source `Observable` instance is not needed.

- `AsyncSubject`: This emits the last value (and only that) emitted by the source `Observable` instance, and only after the source `Observable` instance completes. If the source `Observable` instance does not emit any values, the `AsyncSubject` instance also completes without emitting any values. This is something like a *promise* in RxJava's world. A source `Observable` instance is not needed; the value, the error, or the `OnCompleted` notification can be passed to it by invoking the `on*` methods.

Using subjects may seem a cool way to solve various problems, but you should avoid using them. Or, at least implement them and their behavior in a method that returns a result of type `Observable`.

The danger with the `Subject` instance is that they give access to the `onNext()`, `onError()`, and `onCompleted()` methods, and your logic can get messy (they need to be called following the Rx contract, cited earlier in this chapter). They can be misused very easily.

Opt for using the `ConnecatableObservable` instance (that is, via the `publish()` method) over the `Subject`, when you need to create a hot Observable from a cold one.

But let's look at one good use of a `Subject` instance — the aforementioned *reactive properties*. Again, we are going to implement *'The Reactive Sum'*, but this time it will be quite different. Here is the class defining it:

```
public class ReactiveSum { // (1)
    private BehaviorSubject<Double> a = BehaviorSubject.create(0.0);
    private BehaviorSubject<Double> b = BehaviorSubject.create(0.0);
    private BehaviorSubject<Double> c = BehaviorSubject.create(0.0);
    public ReactiveSum() { // (2)
        Observable.combineLatest(a, b, (x, y) -> x + y).subscribe(c);
    }
    public double getA() { // (3)
        return a.getValue();
    }
    public void setA(double a) {
        this.a.onNext(a);
    }
    public double getB() {
        return b.getValue();
    }
    public void setB(double b) {
        this.b.onNext(b);
    }
```

```
  public double getC() { // (4)
    return c.getValue();
  }
  public Observable<Double> obsC() {
    return c.asObservable();
  }
}
```

This class has three double properties: two settable properties, a and b, and their *sum*, c. When a or b changes, c is *automatically updated* to their sum. There is a special method that we can use to track the changes to c. So how does it work?

1. ReactiveSum is a normal Java class, defining three private fields of type BehaviorSubject<Double>, representing the variables a, b, and c, and with default values of zero.

2. In the constructor, we subscribe c to depend on both a and b and to be equal to their sum, again, using combineLatest() method.

3. The properties a and b have getters and setters. The getters return their current value — the last received value. The setters *emit* the passed value to their Subject instance, making it the last one.

The getValue() method of the BehaviorSubject parameter is used for retrieving it. It is available at RxJava 1.0.5.

4. The property c is read-only, so it has only a getter, but it can be listened to. This can be done with the obsC() method, which returns it as an Observable instance. Remember, when you use subjects, to always encapsulate them in types or methods and return the observables to the outside world.

This ReactiveSum class can be used like this:

```
ReactiveSum sum = new ReactiveSum();
subscribePrint(sum.obsC(), "Sum");
sum.setA(5);
sum.setB(4);
```

This will output the following:

```
Sum : 0.0

Sum : 5.0

Sum : 9.0
```

The first value is *emitted* on the subscribe () method (remember the BehaviorSubject instances always *emit* their last value on subscribing), and the other two will automatically be *emitted* on setting a or b.

 The source code for the preceding example can be viewed/ downloaded at https://github.com/meddle0x53/ learning-rxjava/blob/master/src/main/java/com/ packtpub/reactive/chapter03/ReactiveSumV3.java.

Reactive properties can be used for implementing bindings and counters, so they are very useful for desktop or browser applications. But this example is far from any functional paradigm.

Summary

In this chapter, we've learned many ways of creating different kinds of Observable instances and other related instances (Observer, Subscriber, Subscription, and Subject). We've been creating them from timers, values, collections, and external sources such as files. Using this knowledge as a base, we can begin building logic, by chaining operations to them. Many of the factory methods introduced here we'll be coming back in the next chapters. For example, we will be building different behaviors using the Observable.create method.

In the next chapter, we'll introduce various **operators**, which will give us the power to write real logic using the Observable instances. We have already mentioned some of them, such as map () and filter (), but the time has come to look at them in depth.

Transforming, Filtering, and Accumulating Your Data

4

Now that we have the means for creating `Observable` instances from a wide variety of source data, it's time to build programming logic around these instances. We will present the basic reactive operators that we'll use to achieve step-by-step computations (the reactive way of handling data).

We will begin with transformations, using the famous `flatMap()` and `map()` operators, as well as some more less common transforming operators. After that we'll learn how to filter our data, using the `filter()` operator, skipping elements, receiving only elements at a given position in time. The chapter will also cover accumulating data with the `scan` operator. Most of these operators will be presented using *marble diagrams*.

This chapter covers the following topics:

- Introduction to marble diagrams and transformations with mapping
- Filtering your data
- Accumulating values using the `scan` operator

Observable transformations

We've used the `map()` operator in some of the previous examples. The **higher order functions** which transform the incoming values into something else are called **transformations**. The higher order functions that can be invoked on an `Observable` instance, producing a new `Observable` instance from it, are called operators. The **transforming operators** transform the elements emitted from the source `Observable` instance in some way.

In order to understand how the different operators work, we will be using pictures called **marble diagrams**. For example, this one describes the map operator:

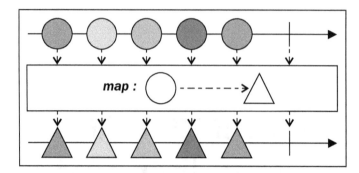

The rectangle in the center of the diagram represents the operator (function). It transforms its input (circles) into something else (triangles). The arrow above the rectangle represents the source Observable instance, the colored circles on it represent OnNext *notifications* emitted in time, and the vertical line at the end is the OnCompleted *notification*. The arrow below the rectangle is the output of the Observable instance with its transformed elements.

So, the map() operator does exactly this: it transforms every '*next*' value from the source to something else, defined via the function passed to it. Here is a little example:

```
Observable<String> mapped = Observable
    .just(2, 3, 5, 8)
    .map(v -> v * 3)
    .map(v -> (v % 2 == 0) ? "even" : "odd");
subscribePrint(mapped, "map");
```

The first map() operator transforms every number emitted from the source to itself, multiplied by three. The second map() operator transforms every multiplied number to a string. The string is 'even' if the number is even and 'odd' otherwise.

Using the map() operator, we can transform each emitted value into a new value. There are more powerful transforming operators that look similar to the map() operator, but have their own usage and purpose. Let's look at them.

Transformations with the various flatMap operators

The flatMap operator is just like the map() operator, but with two differences:

- Instead of receiving a function that transforms a value into an arbitrary type of value, the flatMap operator's argument always transforms a value or sequence of values into the form of an Observable instance.

- It merges the values emitted by those resulting Observable instances. This means that instead of emitting the Observable instances as values it emits their notifications.

Here is the marble diagram for it:

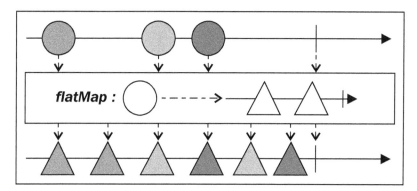

As we can see, each value from the source Observable instance is turned into an Observable instance, and in the end, all the values of these *derivative Observables* are emitted by the resulting Observable instance. Note that the resulting Observable instance may emit the values of the derivative Observable instances in an interleaved fashion and even out of order.

The flatMap operator is very useful for forking logic. For example, if an Observable instance represents a file system folder and emits files from it, we can turn each file object into an Observable instance using the flatMap operator and apply some operations to these *file observables*. The result will be a summary of these operations. Here is an example of reading some files from a folder and dumping them into the standard output:

```
Observable<Path> listFolder(Path dir, String glob) { // (1)
  return Observable.<Path>create(subscriber -> {
    try {
      DirectoryStream<Path> stream = Files.newDirectoryStream(dir,
      glob);
```

```
      subscriber.add(Subscriptions.create(() -> {
        try {
          stream.close();
        }
        catch (IOException e) {
          e.printStackTrace();
        }
      }));
      Observable.<Path>from(stream).subscribe(subscriber);
    }
    catch (DirectoryIteratorException ex) {
      subscriber.onError(ex);
    }
    catch (IOException ioe) {
      subscriber.onError(ioe);
    }
  });
}
Observable<String> from(final Path path) { // (2)
  return Observable.<String>create(subscriber -> {
    try {
      BufferedReader reader = Files.newBufferedReader(path);
      subscriber.add(Subscriptions.create(() -> {
        try {
          reader.close();
        }
        catch (IOException e) {
          e.printStackTrace();
        }
      }));
      String line = null;
      while ((line = reader.readLine()) != null &&
      !subscriber.isUnsubscribed()) {
        subscriber.onNext(line);
      }
      if (!subscriber.isUnsubscribed()) {
        subscriber.onCompleted();
      }
    }
    catch (IOException ioe) {
      if (!subscriber.isUnsubscribed()) {
        subscriber.onError(ioe);
      }
    }
```

```
  });
}
Observable<String> fsObs = listFolder(
  Paths.get("src", "main", "resources"), "{lorem.txt,letters.txt}"
).flatMap(path -> from(path)); // (3)
subscribePrint(fsObs, "FS"); // (4)
```

This piece of code introduces two methods for working with folders and files. We will take a short look at them and how we've used them in this `flatMap` example:

1. The first method, `listFolder()`, takes a folder in the form of a `Path` variable and a `glob` expression. It returns an `Observable` instance representing this folder. This `Observable` instance emits all the files in the folder, complying the `glob` expression as `Path` objects.

    The method is implemented using both the `Observable.create()` and `Observable.from()` operators. The main idea of this implementation is that if an exception occurs, it should be handled and emitted by the resulting `Observable` instance.

    Note the use of the `Subscriber.add()` operator to add a new `Subscription` instance to the subscriber, created using the `Subscriptions.create()` operator. This method creates a `Subscription` instance using an action. This action will be executed when the `Subscription` instance is *unsubscribed*, which means when the `Subscriber` instance is *unsubscribed* in this case. So this is similar to putting the closing of the `stream` in the final block.

2. The other method this example introduces is `Observable<String> from(Path)`.

    It reads a file located and passed to the `path` instance line by line and emits the lines as `OnNext()` *notifications*. The method uses the `Subscriber.add()` operator on a `Subscription` instance for closing the `stream` to the file.

3. The example using `flatMap` creates an `Observable` instance from a folder, using the `listFolder()` operator, which emits two `Path` parameters to files. Using the `flatMap()` operator for every file, we create an `Observable` instance, using the `from(Path)` operator, which emits the file content as lines.

4. The result of the preceding chain will be the two file contents, printed on the standard output. If we used the `Scheduler` instances (see *Chapter 6, Using Concurrency and Parallelism with Schedulers*) for every *file path Observable*, the content would be *scrambled* because the `flatMap` operator interleaves the notifications of the `Observable` instances that it merges.

The source code introducing the Observable<String> from(final Path path) method can be found at https://github.com/meddle0x53/learning-rxjava/blob/724eadf5b0db988b18 5f8d86006d772286037625/src/main/java/com/packtpub/ reactive/common/CreateObservable.java#L61.

The source code containing the Observable<Path> listFolder(Path dir, String glob) method can be viewed/ downloaded at https://github.com/meddle0x53/learning-rxjava/blob/724eadf5b0db988b185f8d86006d772286037625/ src/main/java/com/packtpub/reactive/common/ CreateObservable.java#L128.

The example using the flatMap operator can be viewed/downloaded at https://github.com/meddle0x53/learning-rxjava/blob/ master/src/main/java/com/packtpub/reactive/chapter04/ FlatMapAndFiles.java.

The flatMap operator has multiple overloads. For example, there is one that takes three functions—one for OnNext, one for OnError, and one for OnComleted. It transforms *errors* or *completed* events into Observable instances too, and if there is an OnError or OnCompleted event, their Observable instance transformation is merged in the resulting Observable instance, followed by an OnCompleted *notification*. Here is an example:

```
Observable<Integer> flatMapped = Observable
  .just(-1, 0, 1)
  .map(v -> 2 / v)
  .flatMap(
    v -> Observable.just(v),
    e -> Observable.just(0),
    () -> Observable.just(42)
  );
subscribePrint(flatMapped, "flatMap");
```

The output of that will be -2 (2/-1) and 0 (because of the error raised by 2/0). Because of the *error*, 1 won't be emitted and won't reach the flatMap operator.

Another interesting overload is `Observable<R> flatMap(Func1<T, Observable<U>>, Func2<T, U, R>)`. Here is its marble diagram:

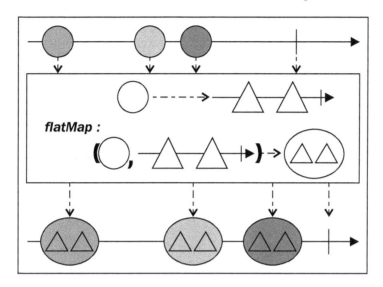

This one combines items from the source `Observable` instance with the `Observable` instance triggered by those source items and calls a user-supplied function with the pair of the original and derived items. The `Observable` instance will then emit the result of this function. Here is an example:

```
Observable<Integer> flatMapped = Observable
.just(5, 432)
.flatMap(
  v -> Observable.range(v, 2),
  (x, y) -> x + y);
subscribePrint(flatMapped, "flatMap");
```

The output is:

flatMap : 10

flatMap : 11

flatMap : 864

flatMap : 865

flatMap ended!

This is because the first element emitted by the source Observable instance is 5, the flatMap operator turns it into an Observable instance using the range() operator, which emits 5 and 6. But this flatMap operator doesn't stop here; for every item emitted by this range Observable instance, it applies the second function with first parameter — the original item (5) and second parameter — the range-emitted item. So we have 5 + 5 and then 5 + 6. The same is applied for the second item emitted by the source Observable instance: 432. It is turned to 432 + 432 = 864 and 432 + 433 = 865.

This overload is useful when all of the derivative items need to have access to their source item and usually saves us from using some kind of **tuple** or **pair** classes, saving on memory and library dependencies. In the earlier example with files, we could prepend the name of the file to each of the outputted lines:

```
CreateObservable.listFolder(
    Paths.get("src", "main", "resources"),
    "{lorem.txt,letters.txt}"
).flatMap(
    path -> CreateObservable.from(path),
    (path, line) -> path.getFileName() + " : " + line
);
```

The operator flatMapIterable doesn't take as parameter lambda that takes arbitrary value as a parameter and returns an Observable instance. Instead the lambda passed to it takes arbitrary value and returns an Iterable instance. All of these Iterable instances are flattened to values emitted by the resulting Observable instance. Let's take a look at the following code snippet:

```
Observable<?> fIterableMapped = Observable
.just(
    Arrays.asList(2, 4),
    Arrays.asList("two", "four"),
)
.flatMapIterable(l -> l);
```

This simple example merges the two lists emitted by the source Observable instance, and the result emits the four items. It is worth mentioning that invoking flatMapIterable(list -> list) is the same as invoking flatMap(l → Observable.from(l)).

Another form of the `flatMap` operator is the `concatMap` operator. It behaves just like the original `flatMap` operator, except that it concatenates rather than merges the resulting `Observable` instance in order to generate its own sequence. The following marble diagram shows how it works:

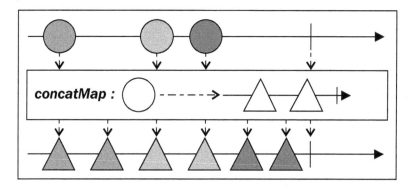

The items from the different *derivative Observables* are not interleaved, as with the `flatMap` operator. A significant difference between the `flatMap` and `concatMap` operators is that the `flatMap` operator uses the inner `Observable` instances in parallel, whereas the `concatMap` operator only subscribes to one of the `Observable` instances at a time.

The last operator similar to `flatMap` is `switchMap`. Its marble diagram looks like this:

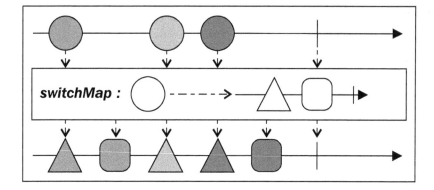

It operates in similar fashion to the `flatMap` operator, except that whenever a new item is emitted by the source `Observable` instance, it stops mirroring the `Observable` instance generated from the previously emitted item and it begins mirroring only the current `Observable` instance. In other words, it internally unsubscribes from the current *derivative* `Observable` instance when the next one begins emitting its items. Here is an example of this:

```
Observable<Object> obs = Observable
.interval(40L, TimeUnit.MILLISECONDS)
.switchMap(v ->
  Observable
  .timer(0L, 10L, TimeUnit.MILLISECONDS)
  .map(u -> "Observable <" + (v + 1) + "> : " + (v + u)))
);
subscribePrint(obs, "switchMap");
```

The source `Observable` instance is using the `Observable.interval()` operator to emit sequential numbers (beginning with zero) every 40 milliseconds. Using the `switchMap` operator, a new `Observable` instance emitting another sequence of numbers is created for every number. This secondary sequence of numbers begins from the source number that was passed to the `switchMap` operator (that's implemented by summing the source number with every emitted number, using the `map()` operator). So, every 40 milliseconds, a new sequence of numbers is being emitted (each number at 10-millisecond intervals).

The resulting output looks like:

```
switchMap : Observable <1> : 0
switchMap : Observable <1> : 1
switchMap : Observable <1> : 2
switchMap : Observable <1> : 3
switchMap : Observable <2> : 1
switchMap : Observable <2> : 2
switchMap : Observable <2> : 3
switchMap : Observable <2> : 4
switchMap : Observable <3> : 2
switchMap : Observable <3> : 3
switchMap : Observable <3> : 4
switchMap : Observable <3> : 5
switchMap : Observable <3> : 6
switchMap : Observable <4> : 3
. . . . . . . . . . . . . . . . .
```

The source code for all the mapping examples can be downloaded/
viewed at https://github.com/meddle0x53/learning-
rxjava/blob/master/src/main/java/com/packtpub/
reactive/chapter04/MappingExamples.java.

Grouping items

Items can be grouped by specific property or key.

First, we'll look at the groupBy() operator, a method that divides a source
Observable instance into multiple Observable instances. Each of these Observable
instances emits some of the source's items depending on a grouping function.

The groupBy() operator returns an Observable instance that emits
Observable instances. These Observable instances are special; they are of type
GroupedObservable, and you can retrieve their grouping keys using the getKey()
method. Once the groupBy() operator is used, the different groups can be handled
in a different or a common way.

Note that when the groupBy() operator creates an observable that emits the
GroupedObservables instances, each of them buffers its items. So, if we ignore
any of them, this buffer will present a potential memory leak.

The marble diagram of the groupBy() operator looks like this:

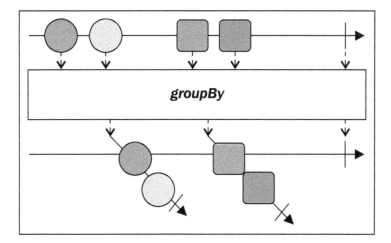

Here, the form of the items is used as the common trait of the grouping. For a better understanding of the idea of the method, we can look at this example:

```
List<String> albums = Arrays.asList(
  "The Piper at the Gates of Dawn",
  "A Saucerful of Secrets",
  "More", "Ummagumma", "Atom Heart Mother",
  "Meddle", "Obscured by Clouds",
  "The Dark Side of the Moon",
  "Wish You Were Here", "Animals", "The Wall"
);
Observable
  .from(albums)
  .groupBy(album -> album.split(" ").length)
  .subscribe(obs ->
    subscribePrint(obs, obs.getKey() + " word(s)")
  );
```

The example emits some of Pink Floyd's album titles and groups them by the number of words contained in them. For example `Meddle` and `More` are in the same group with key `1`, and `A Saucerful of Secrets` and `Wish You Were Here` are both in a group with the key of `4`. All these groups are presented by the `GroupedObservable` instances, so we can subscribe to them in the `subscribe()` call of the source `Observable` instance. The different groups are printed with different labels, depending on their keys. The output of this little program is as follows:

```
7 word(s) : The Piper at the Gates of Dawn

4 word(s) : A Saucerful of Secrets

1 word(s) : More

1 word(s) : Ummagumma

3 word(s) : Atom Heart Mother

1 word(s) : Meddle

3 word(s) : Obscured by Clouds

6 word(s) : The Dark Side of the Moon

4 word(s) : Wish You Were Here

1 word(s) : Animals

2 word(s) : The Wall
```

The order the items are emitted in is the same, but they are emitted by different `GroupedObservable` instances. Also, all the `GroupedObservable` instances are completed after the source completes.

The `groupBy()` operator has another overload that takes a second, transforming function that transforms each of the items in a group in some way. Here is an example:

```
Observable
.from(albums)
.groupBy(
  album -> album.replaceAll("[^mM]", "").length(),
  album -> album.replaceAll("[mM]", "*")
)
.subscribe(
  obs -> subscribePrint(obs, obs.getKey()+" occurences of 'm'")
);
```

The album titles are grouped by the number of the occurrences of the letter m in them. The text is transformed in a way that all the occurrences of the letter are replaced with *. The output is as follows:

```
0 occurences of 'm' : The Piper at the Gates of Dawn

0 occurences of 'm' : A Saucerful of Secrets

1 occurences of 'm' : *ore

4 occurences of 'm' : U**agu**a

2 occurences of 'm' : Ato* Heart *other

1 occurences of 'm' : *eddle

0 occurences of 'm' : Obscured by Clouds

1 occurences of 'm' : The Dark Side of the *oon

0 occurences of 'm' : Wish You Were Here

1 occurences of 'm' : Ani*als

0 occurences of 'm' : The Wall
```

 The source code demonstrating use of the `Observable.groupBy()` operator can be found at`https://github.com/meddle0x53/learning-rxjava/blob/master/src/main/java/com/packtpub/reactive/chapter04/UsingGroupBy.java`.

Additional useful transformation operators

There are a few additional *transformations* worth mentioning. For example, there is the `cast()` operator, which is a shortcut for the `map(v -> someClass.cast(v))`.

```
List<Number> list = Arrays.asList(1, 2, 3);
Observable<Integer> iObs = Observable
    .from(list)
    .cast(Integer.class);
```

The initial `Observable` instance here emits values of type `Number`, but they are actually `Integer` instances, so we can use the `cast()` operator to represent them as `Integer` instances.

Another helpful operator is the `timestamp()` operator. It adds a *timestamp* to each emitted value by transforming it into an instance of the `Timestamped<T>` class. This is helpful if, for example, we want to log the output of an `Observable`, as follows:

```
List<Number> list = Arrays.asList(3, 2);
Observable<Timestamped<Number>> timestamp = Observable
    .from(list)
    .timestamp();
subscribePrint(timestamp, "Timestamps");
```

In this example, each number is being timestamped. Again, that can be implemented using the `map()` operator very easily. The output of the preceding example looks like this:

```
Timestamps : Timestamped(timestampMillis = 1431184924388, value = 1)
Timestamps : Timestamped(timestampMillis = 1431184924394, value = 2)
Timestamps : Timestamped(timestampMillis = 1431184924394, value = 3)
```

A similar operator is the `timeInterval` operator, but it transforms a value to an instance of the `TimeInterval<T>` operator instead. A `TimeInterval<T>` instance represents an item emitted by an `Observable` along with the amount of time that elapsed either since the emission of the previous item, or (if there was no previous item) since the subscription. This can be used for generating statistics, for example:

```
Observable<TimeInterval<Long>> timeInterval = Observable
    .timer(0L, 150L, TimeUnit.MILLISECONDS)
    .timeInterval();
subscribePrint(timeInterval, "Time intervals");
```

This will output something similar to this:

```
Time intervals : TimeInterval [intervalInMilliseconds=13, value=0]
Time intervals : TimeInterval [intervalInMilliseconds=142, value=1]
Time intervals : TimeInterval [intervalInMilliseconds=149, value=2]
```

. . . .

We can see that the different values are emitted roughly at 150 milliseconds, as they should be.

Both the `timeInterval` and `timestamp` operators work on the *immediate* scheduler (see *Chapter 6, Using Concurrency and Parallelism with Schedulers*), and both of them keep their time information in milliseconds.

 The source code for the preceding examples can be found at https://github.com/meddle0x53/learning-rxjava/blob/master/src/main/java/com/packtpub/reactive/chapter04/VariousTransformationsDemonstration.java.

Filtering data

In the first chapter's reactive sum example, we were filtering the user input, based on a special pattern. The pattern was, for example, *a: <number>*. It is common to filter only interesting bits of data from the data stream. For example, it's useful to filter out *<enter>* key-down events only from all key-down events, or only lines containing a given expression from a file. That's why it is important to not only be able to transform our data but also to learn how to filter it.

There are many filtering operators in RxJava. The most important of these operators is `filter()`. Its marble diagram is very simple and is shown here:

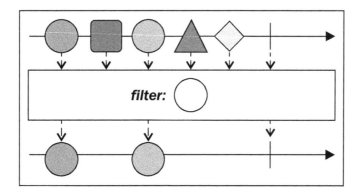

It shows that the `filter()` operator filters the data by some property. In the diagram, it's the form of the elements: it filters only circles. Like all the other operators, `filter()` creates a new `Observable` instance from the source. This `Observable` instance emits only items that comply to the condition, defined by the `filter()` operator. The following piece of code illustrates that:

```
Observable<Integer> numbers = Observable
    .just(1, 13, 32, 45, 21, 8, 98, 103, 55);
Observable<Integer> filter = numbers
    .filter(n -> n % 2 == 0);
subscribePrint(filter, "Filter");
```

This will output only *even* numbers (32, 8, and 98), because of the filtering condition.

The `filter()` operator filters elements based on a user-defined function. There are quite a few additional filtering operators. In order to understand them, let's look at some simple examples:

```
Observable<Integer> numbers = Observable
    .just(1, 13, 32, 45, 21, 8, 98, 103, 55);
Observable<String> words = Observable
    .just(
        "One", "of", "the", "few", "of",
        "the", "crew", "crew"
    );
Observable<?> various = Observable
    .from(Arrays.asList("1", 2, 3.0, 4, 5L));
```

We define three `Observable` instances to use in our examples. The first one emits nine numbers. The second one emits all the words from a sentence, one by one. The third one emits elements of different types—strings, integers, doubles, and longs.

```
subscribePrint(numbers.takeLast(4), "Last 4");
```

The `takeLast()` operator returns a new `Observable` instance that emits only the last *n* items from the source `Observable` instance, only when it completes. This method has a few overloads. For example, there is one that emits the last *N* or less items from the source, emitted in a specified time window. Another one can receive a `Scheduler` instance in order to be executed on another thread.

In this example, only the last four items of the `Observable` instance will be filtered and output:

Last 4 : 8

Last 4 : 98

Last 4 : 103

Last 4 : 55

Last 4 ended!

Let's take a look at the following code snippet:

```
subscribePrint(numbers.last(), "Last");
```

The `Observable` instance created by the `last()` operator, which outputs only the *last item* emitted by the source `Observable` instance when it completes. If the source doesn't emit an item, a `NoSuchElementException` exception will be emitted as an `OnError()` *notification*. It has an overload that receives a predicate parameter of type `T->Boolean`. As a result, it emits only the last item emitted by the source, complying to the condition defined by the predicate. In this example, the output will be as follows:

Last : 55

Last ended!

The `takeLastBuffer()` method behaves much like the `takeLast()` method, but the `Observable` instance created by it emits only one item—a `List` instance containing the last *N* items from the source:

```
subscribePrint(
    numbers.takeLastBuffer(4), "Last buffer"
);
```

It has analogical overloads to the `takeLast()` method's. The output here is as follows:

Last buffer : [8, 98, 103, 55]

Last buffer ended!

The `lastOrDefault()` operator behaves like and has the same overload with a predicate as the `last()` operator:

```
subscribePrint(
    numbers.lastOrDefault(200), "Last or default"
);
subscribePrint(
    Observable.empty().lastOrDefault(200), "Last or default"
);
```

However, if the source doesn't emit anything, the `lastOrDefault()` operator emits the default value instead of the `OnError` *notification*. The output of this example is as follows:

```
Last or default : 55

Last or default ended!

Last or default : 200

Last or default ended!
```

The `skipLast()` operator is the exact opposite of the `takeLast()` method; it emits everything except the last *N* items from the source when it completes:

```
subscribePrint(numbers.skipLast(4), "Skip last 4");
```

It has similar overloads. The output of this example is as follows:

```
Skip last 4 : 1

Skip last 4 : 13
```

The `skip()` method is the same as the `skipLast()` method but skips the first *N* items instead of the last:

```
subscribePrint(numbers.skip(4), "Skip 4");
```

This means that the output of the example is as follows:

```
Skip 4 : 21

Skip 4 : 8

Skip 4 : 98

Skip 4 : 103

Skip 4 : 55

Skip 4 ended!
```

The `take()` operator is similar to the `takeLast()` operator, but instead of the last *N* items of the source, it emits the first *N* items.

```
subscribePrint(numbers.take(4), "First 4");
```

This is a commonly-used operator, cheaper than the `takeLast()` operator, because the `takeLast()` operator buffers its items and waits for the source to complete. This operator doesn't buffer its items but emits them when it receives them. It is very useful for limiting infinite `Observable` instances. The output of the preceding example is as follows:

```
First 4 : 1

First 4 : 13
```

```
First 4 : 32
First 4 : 45
First 4 ended!
```

Let's take a look at the following code snippet:

```
subscribePrint(numbers.first(), "First");
```

The `first()` operator is similar to the `last()` operator but emits only the first item emitted by the source. It emits the same `OnError` *notification* if there is no first item. Its predicate form has an alias— the `takeFirst()` operator. There is also a `firstOrDefault()` operator form of this operator. The output of this example is clear:

```
First : 1
First ended!
```

Let's take a look at the following code snippet:

```
subscribePrint(numbers.elementAt(5), "At 5");
```

The `elementAt()` operator is similar to the `first()` and `last()` operators but has no predicate form. There is an `elementAtOrDefault()` form though. It emits only the element at the specified index in the sequence of items, emitted by the source `Observable` instance. This example outputs the following:

```
At 5 : 8
At 5 ended!
```

Let's take a look at the following code snippet:

```
subscribePrint(words.distinct(), "Distinct");
```

The `Observable` instance produced by the `distinct()` operator emits the items from the source, excluding the repeated ones. There is an overload that can receive a function, returning a key or hash code value to be used to decide whether an item is distinct from another or not:

```
Distinct : One
Distinct : of
Distinct : the
Distinct : few
Distinct : crew
Distinct ended!
```

```
  subscribePrint(
    words.distinctUntilChanged(), "Distinct until changed"
  );
```

The `distinctUntilChanged()` operator is similar to the `distinct()` method, but the `Observable` instance that it returns emits all items emitted by the source `Observable` instance that are distinct from their immediate predecessors. So, in this example, it will emit every word, except the last one, `crew`.

```
  subscribePrint( // (13)
    various.ofType(Integer.class), "Only integers"
  );
```

The `ofType()` operator creates an `Observable` instance that emits only the items emitted by the source of a given type. It basically is a shortcut to this call: `filter(v -> Class.isInstance(v))`. In this example the output will be as follows:

Only integers : 2

Only integers : 4

Only integers ended!

> The source code for all of these examples can be viewed/downloaded at `https://github.com/meddle0x53/learning-rxjava/blob/master/src/main/java/com/packtpub/reactive/chapter04/FilteringExamples.java`.

These are the most commonly used *filtering* operators provided by RxJava. We'll be using some of them a lot in later examples.

The `last` operator we'll look at in this chapter is a transformational one, but a bit special. It can use previously accumulated states! Let's learn more about it.

Accumulating data

The scan(Func2) operator takes a function with two arguments as a parameter. Its result is an Observable instance. The first item, emitted by the result of the scan() method, is the first item of the source Observable instance. The second item emitted is created by applying the function that was passed to the scan() method on the previous item emitted by the result Observable instance and the second item, emitted by the source Observable instance. The third item, emitted by the scan() method result, is created by applying the function, passed to the scan() method to the previous item, emitted by it and the third item emitted by the source Observable instance. This pattern continues in order to create the rest of the sequence emitted by the Observable instance creates by the scan() method. The function passed to the scan() method is called an **accumulator**.

Let's look at the marble diagram of the scan(Func2) method:

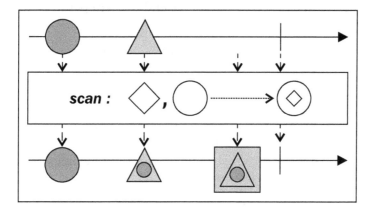

The items emitted by the scan() method can be generated using an accumulated state. In the diagram, the circle is accumulated in the triangle, and then this triangle-circle is accumulated in the square.

This means that we can emit the sums of a sequence of integers, for example:

```
Observable<Integer> scan = Observable
    .range(1, 10)
    .scan((p, v) -> p + v);
subscribePrint(scan, "Sum");
subscribePrint(scan.last(), "Final sum");
```

The first *subscription* will output all the emissions : *1, 3 (1+2), 6 (3 + 3), 10 (6 + 4) .. 55*. But in most cases, we are interested only in the last emitted item—the final sum. We can use an `Observable` instance that emits only the last element, using the `last()` filtering operator. It's worth mentioning that there is a `reduce(Func2)` operator, an alias for the `scan(Func2).last()`.

The `scan()` operator has one overload which can be used with a *seed/initial* parameter. In this case, the function passed to the `scan(T, Func2)` operator is applied to the first item emitted by the source and this *seed* parameter.

```
Observable<String> file = CreateObservable.from(
    Paths.get("src", "main", "resources", "letters.txt")
);
scan = file.scan(0, (p, v) -> p + 1);
subscribePrint(scan.last(), "wc -l");
```

This example counts the number of lines in a file. The file `Observable` instance emits the lines of the file specified by the given path, one-by-one. We use the `scan(T, Func2)` operator with a *seed* value of `0` to count the lines by adding one to the accumulated count on every line.

We will conclude this chapter with an example using many of the operators introduced in it, together. Let's look at it:

```
Observable<String> file = CreateObservable.from(
    Paths.get("src", "main", "resources", "operators.txt")
);
Observable<String> multy = file
    .flatMap(line -> Observable.from(line.split("\\."))) // (1)
    .map(String::trim) // (2)
    .map(sentence -> sentence.split(" ")) // (3)
    .filter(array -> array.length > 0) // (4)
    .map(array -> array[0]) // (5)
    .distinct() // (6)
    .groupBy(word -> word.contains("'")) //(7)
    .flatMap(observable -> observable.getKey() ? observable : // (8)
      observable.map(Introspector::decapitalize))
```

```
    .map(String::trim) // (9)
    .filter(word -> !word.isEmpty()) // (10)
    .scan((current, word) -> current + " " + word) // (11)
    .last() // (12)
    .map(sentence -> sentence + "."); // (13)
subscribePrint(multy, "Multiple operators"); // (14)
```

This piece of code uses lots of operators to filter out and assemble a sentence hidden in a file. The file is represented by an `Observable` instance, which emits all the lines contained in it one by one.

1. We don't want to operate only on the different lines; we want to emit all the sentences contained in the file. So, we use the `flatMap` operator to create an `Observable` instance which emits the file sentences by sentence (determined by `dot`).

2. We trim these sentences using the `map()` operator. It is possible for them to contain some leading or trailing spaces.

3. We want to operate on the different words contained in our sentence items, so we turn them into arrays of words, using the `map()` operator and the `String::split` parameter.

4. We don't care about empty sentences (if there are any), so we filter them out using the `filter()` operator.

5. We need only the first words from the sentences, so we use the `map()` operator to get them. The resulting `Observable` instance emits the first word of every sentence contained in the file.

6. We don't need duplicated words, so we use the `distinct()` operator to get rid of them.

7. Now we want to branch our logic in a way that some of the words are treated differently. So we use the `groupBy()` operator and a `Boolean` key to divide our words into two `Observable` instances. The key is `True` for the chosen words and `False` for all the others.

8. Using the `flatMap` operator, we join our separated words, but only the chosen ones (with a key of `True`) are left unchanged. The rest are *decapitalized*.

9. We trim all the different words from leading/trailing spaces, using the `map()` operator.

10. We use the `filter()` operator to filter out the empty ones.

11. Using the `scan()` operator, we concatenate the words with spaces as separators.

12. With the `last()` operator, our resulting `Observable` instance will emit only the last concatenation, containing all the words.

13. One last call to the `map()` operator creates a sentence from our concatenated words by adding a dot.

14. If we output the single item emitted by this `Observable` instance, we'll get a sentence composed of the first words of all the sentences contained in the initial file (skipping duplicated words)!

And the output is as follows:

```
Multiple operators : I'm the one who will become RX.
Multiple operators ended!
```

> The preceding example can be found at https://github.com/meddle0x53/learning-rxjava/blob/master/src/main/java/com/packtpub/reactive/chapter04/VariousTransformationsDemonstration.java.

Summary

The example concluding the chapter demonstrates what we've learned so far. We can write complex logic by chaining the `Observable` instances using a variety of operators. We can transform incoming data using the `map()` or `flatMap()` operators and can branch logic by using the `groupBy()` or `filter()` operators or the different `flatMap()` operators. We can join these branches again with the `flatMap()` operators. We can select parts of the data with the help of different filters and accumulate it with the `scan()` operator. Using all of these operators, we can write pretty decent programs in a readable and simple way. The complexity of the program doesn't affect the complexity of the code.

The next step is to learn how to combine the branches of our logic in a more straightforward fashion. We'll learn how to combine data coming from different sources too. So let's proceed with the next chapter!

5
Combinators, Conditionals, and Error Handling

Most of the programs that we write handle data from different sources. These sources can be both external (files, databases, servers, and many others) and internal (different collections or branches of the same external source). There are many cases in which we'll want to have these sources depend on each other in one way or another. Defining these dependencies is a necessary step in building our programs. The idea of this chapter is to introduce the `Observable` operators capable of that.

We saw an example of combined `Observable` instances in the first and second chapters. Our "Reactive Sum" program had one external data source — the user input but it branched it into two internal data sources, depending on the custom format. We saw how we can use the `filter()` operator instead of procedural `if-else` constructions. Later, we combined these data flows into one, with the help of a combinator.

We'll learn how to react to errors from inside the `Observable` instance chain. Remember, being able to react to failures makes our programs resilient.

In this chapter we will cover:

- Combining the `Observable` instances using operators such as `combineLatest()`, `merge()`, `concat()`, and `zip()`
- Creating dependencies between the `Observable` instances using conditional operators such as `takeUntil()`, `skipUntil()`, and `amb()`
- Error handling using operators such as `retry()`, `onErrorResumeNext()`, and `onErrorReturn()`

Combining the Observable instances

We'll first look at the `zip(Observable, Observable, <Observable>..., Func)` operator, which can *combine* two or more `Observable` instances using a *combining* function.

The zip operator

The function passed to the `zip` operator has as many parameters as the number of the `Observable` instances passed to the `zip()` method. When all of these `Observable` instances emit at least one item, the function is called with the parameter values first emitted by each of the `Observable` instances. Its result will be the first emitted item by the `Observable` instance created via the `zip()` method. The second item emitted by this `Observable` instance will be a combination (computed using the function parameter of the `zip()` method) of the second items of the source `Observable` instances. Even if one of the source `Observable` instances has emitted three or more items, its second emitted item is used. The resulting `Observable` instance always emits the same number of items as the source `Observable` instance, which emits the fewest items and then completes.

This behavior can be better seen in this marble diagram:

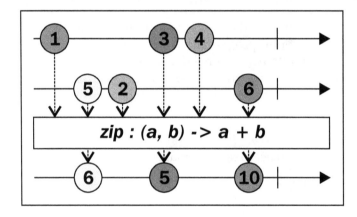

Here is a very simple example of using the `zip()` method:

```
Observable<Integer> zip = Observable
.zip(
  Observable.just(1, 3, 4),
  Observable.just(5, 2, 6),
  (a, b) -> a + b
);
subscribePrint(zip, "Simple zip");
```

The example is similar to the marble diagram and outputs the same result. The first item emitted by the Observable instance created by the zip() method is emitted by the time all of the sources have emitted at least one item. This means that even if one of the sources emits all of its items, the result will be emitted only when all of the other sources emit items.

Now if you remember the interval() operator from *Chapter 3, Creating and Connecting Observables, Observers, and Subjects*, it is able to create an Observable instance emitting sequential numbers every <n> milliseconds. What if you want to emit a sequence of, say, arbitrary objects instead? This is possible by combining the interval() and from() or just() methods using the zip() method. Let's look at an example of that:

```
Observable<String> timedZip = Observable
.zip(
  Observable.from(Arrays.asList("Z", "I", "P", "P")),
  Observable.interval(300L, TimeUnit.MILLISECONDS),
  (value, i) -> value
);
subscribePrint(timedZip, "Timed zip");
```

This will output Z after 300 milliseconds, I after another 300 milliseconds, P after the same interval , and another P after 300 more milliseconds. After that, the timedZip Observable instance will complete. That's because the source Observable instance, created via the interval() method emits, its element every 300 milliseconds, and it determines the speed of the timedZip parameter emissions.

The zip() method has an instance method version too. The operator is called zipWith(). Here is an analogous example to the preceding one but using the zipWith() operator:

```
Observable<String> timedZip = Observable
.from(Arrays.asList("Z", "I", "P", "P"))
.zipWith(
  Observable.interval(300L, TimeUnit.MILLISECONDS),
  (value, skip) -> value
);
subscribePrint(timedZip, "Timed zip");
```

Next, we'll get to know the *combinator* we first saw in *Chapter 1, An Introduction to Reactive Programming*, while implementing *'The Reactive Sum'*.

The combineLatest operator

The `combineLatest()` operator has the same parameters and overloads as the `zip()` operator but behaves a bit differently. The `Observable` instance it creates emits the first item as soon as there is at least one of each source, taking the last of each. After that, the `Observable` instance it creates emits an item whenever any of the source `Observable` instances emits an item. The number of items emitted by the `combineLatest()` operator depends entirely on the order of items emitted, since multiple items could be emitted from a single source before there is one of each source. Its marble diagram looks like this:

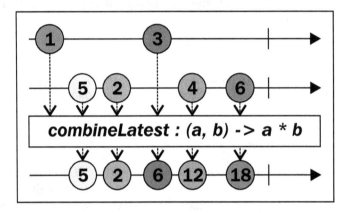

In the preceding diagram, the color of the items emitted by the combining `Observable` instance are the same as the colors of those items triggering their emission.

In the next few examples, will be using three source `Observable` instances, created by the `interval()` and `zipWith()` methods:

```
Observable<String> greetings = Observable
.just("Hello", "Hi", "Howdy", "Zdravei", "Yo", "Good to see ya")
.zipWith(
  Observable.interval(1L, TimeUnit.SECONDS),
  this::onlyFirstArg
);
Observable<String> names = Observable
.just("Meddle", "Tanya", "Dali", "Joshua")
.zipWith(
  Observable.interval(1500L, TimeUnit.MILLISECONDS),
  this::onlyFirstArg
);
```

```
Observable<String> punctuation = Observable
.just(".", "?", "!", "!!!", "...")
.zipWith(
  Observable.interval(1100L, TimeUnit.MILLISECONDS),
  this::onlyFirstArg
);
```

This is the function used for zipping:

```
public <T, R> T onlyFirstArg(T arg1, R arg2) {
  return arg1;
}
```

This is the same method of inserting delays between emissions as seen in the section about the `zip()` method. These three `Observable` instances can be used to compare the different combining methods. The `Observable` instance containing greetings emits every second, the one containing names emits every second and a half, and the one with punctuation signs every 1.1 seconds.

Using the `combineLatest()` operator, we can combine them like this:

```
Observable<String> combined = Observable
.combineLatest(
  greetings, names, punctuation,
  (greeting, name, puntuation) ->
    greeting + " " + name + puntuation)
;
subscribePrint(combined, "Sentences");
```

This will combine the different source items in sentences. The first sentence will be emitted after a second and a half because all the sources have to emit something in order for the combined `Observable` instance to start its emissions. This sentence will be 'Hello Meddle.'. The next sentence will be emitted the moment any of the sources emits something. This will happen two seconds after subscribing, because the greetings `Observable` instance emits every second; it will emit 'Hi', and this will make the combined `Observable` instance emit 'Hi Meddle.'. When 2.2 seconds pass, the punctuation `Observable` instance will emit '?', so we'll have another sentence— 'Hi Meddle?'. This will continue until all of the sources are completed.

The `combineLatest()` operator is very useful when we need computation or notification when any of the data sources we depend on changes. The next method is simpler; it just merges the emissions of its sources, *interleaving* them in the process.

The merge operator

When we want to get feeds from multiple sources as one stream, we can use the merge() operator. For example, we can have many Observable instances emitting data from different log files. We don't care which log file is the source of the current emission, we just want to see all the logs.

The diagram of the merge() operator is pretty simple:

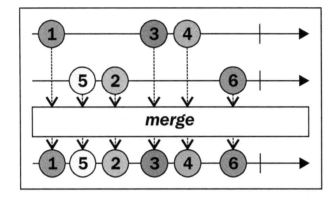

Every item is emitted at its original emission time, and the source doesn't matter. An example using the three Observable instances introduced in the previous section looks like this:

```
Observable<String> merged = Observable
    .merge(greetings, names, punctuation);
subscribePrint(merged, "Words");
```

It just emits different words/punctuation signs. The first word emitted will come from the greetings Observable instance, one second after the subscription (because greetings emits every second) 'Hello'; then '.' will be emitted after 100 milliseconds because the punctuation Observable instance emits its items every 1.1 seconds. After 400 milliseconds, one second and a half after the subscription, 'Meddle' will be emitted. Next is the greeting 'Hi'. Emissions will continue to take place until the source Observable instance, which takes the most time, completes.

It is worth mentioning that if any of the sources emits an OnError notification, the merge Observable instance emits the *error* too and completes with it. There is a form of merge() operator that delays emitting errors until all the error-free source Observable instances are completed. It is called mergeDelayError().

If we want to combine our sources in such a way that their items don't interleave in time and the emissions of the first passed source take precedence over the next one, we will be using the last combinator that this chapter introduces — the `concat()` operator.

The concat operator

All of the chapters in this book are in different files. We want to concatenate the content of all of these files into one big file, representing the whole book. We can create an `Observable` instance for each chapter-file with the `from(Path)` method that we created earlier, and we can use the `concat()` operator with these `Observable` instances as sources to concatenate them in the right order in one `Observable` instance. If we subscribe to this `Observable` instance with a method that writes everything in a file, we'll have our book-file in the end.

Note that the `conact()` operator won't work well with infinite `Observable` instances. It will emit the notifications of the first one, but it will block the others. The main difference between the `merge()` and `concat()` operators is that `merge()` subscribes to all source `Observable` instances at the same time, whereas `concat()` has exactly one subscription at any time.

The marble diagram of the `concat()` operator looks like this:

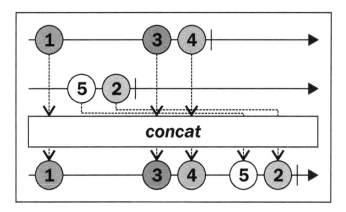

Here is an example of concatenating the three `Observable` instances from the previous examples:

```
Observable<String> concat = Observable
    .concat(greetings, names, punctuation);
subscribePrint(concat, "Concat");
```

This will output all of the greetings, one by one, every second, then the names every second and a half, and finally the punctuation signs every 1.1 seconds. Between the greetings and the names there will be a second and a half.

There is one operator, similar to the `concat()` operator, called `startWith()`. It prepends items to an `Observable` instance and has overloads that take one, two, three, and so on, up to nine values, with an `Iterable` instance or another `Observable` instance. Using the overload taking another `Observable` instance as a parameter, we can simulate the `concat()` operator. Here is the preceding example implemented in the following code:

```
Observable<String> concat = punctuation
    .startWith(names)
    .startWith(greetings);
subscribePrint(concat, "Concatenated");
```

The greetings `Observable` instance is prepended to the names one, and the result of this is prepended to the punctuation of the `Observable` instance, creating the same `Observable` instance of concatenated sources as in the preceding example.

> The source code for the preceding and all the previous examples in this chapter can be found at `https://github.com/meddle0x53/learning-rxjava/blob/master/src/main/java/com/packtpub/reactive/chapter05/CombiningObservables.java`.

Good use of the `startWith()` operator is when it is used with the `combineLatest()` operator. If you remember the initial implementation of our *'Reactive Sum'* example, you had to enter both the a and b values in order to calculate the initial sum. But suppose we modify the construction of the sum like this:

```
Observable.combineLatest(
    a.startWith(0.0),
    b.startWith(0.0),
    (x, y) -> x + y
);
```

We will have an initial sum of `0.0` even before the user has entered anything and the situation in which the user has entered a for the first time and not yet gave value to b in which case we don't see the sum won't occur.

Again, like with the `merge()` operator, the `concat()` operator has an instance form — the `concatWith()` operator.

In this section of the chapter, we saw how we can combine different Observable instances. But combining is not the only interaction between the Observable instances. They can depend on each other or manage each other. There is a way of getting one or more Observable instances to create conditions changing the behavior of other Observable instances. It's achieved through conditional operator/operators.

The conditional operators

It is possible to make it so that one Observable instance won't begin its emissions until another emits, or so that it would emit only if another doesn't emit anything. These Observable instances are able to emit items under given conditions, and these conditions are applied to them using *conditional* operators. In this section, we'll take a look at some of the *conditional* operators provided by RxJava.

The amb operator

The amb() operator has overloads that take from two up to nine source Observable instances or an Iterable instance of the Observable instances. It emits the items of the source Observable instance that starts emitting first. It doesn't matter what this is, whether OnError, OnCompleted notification, or data. Its diagram looks like this:

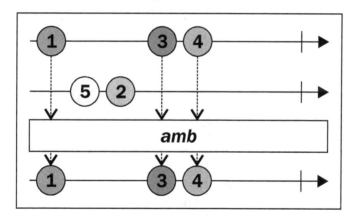

This operator has an instance form too. It is called ambWith() and can be called on one Observable instance in argument with another Observable instance.

This *conditional* operator is good for reading from multiple sources of similar data. The subscriber won't care about the origin of the data. It can be used to implement simple caching, for example. Here is a little example of how it may be used:

```
Observable<String> words = Observable.just("Some", "Other");
Observable<Long> interval = Observable
    .interval(500L, TimeUnit.MILLISECONDS)
    .take(2);
subscribePrint(Observable.amb(words, interval), "Amb 1");
Random r = new Random();
Observable<String> source1 = Observable
    .just("data from source 1")
    .delay(r.nextInt(1000), TimeUnit.MILLISECONDS);
Observable<String> source2 = Observable
    .just("data from source 2")
    .delay(r.nextInt(1000), TimeUnit.MILLISECONDS);
subscribePrint(Observable.amb(source1, source2), "Amb 2");
```

The first amb() operator will emit the items of the *words* Observable instance, because the *interval* Observable instance will have to wait for half a second before emitting, and the *words* will begin emitting immediately.

The emission of the second amb Observable instance will be decided at random. If the first source Observable instance emits its data before the second, its emission will be mirrored by the amb Observable instance, but if the second source emits first, the amb Observable instance will emit its data.

The takeUntil(), takeWhile(), skipUntil(), and skipWhile() conditional operators

We saw operators similar to these in the previous chapter. The take(int) operator filtered only the first *n* items. These operators also filter items, but *based on conditions*. The takeUntil() operator takes another Observable instance, and until this other Observable instance emits, the source's items are emitted; after that, the Observable instance created by the takeUntil() operator completes. Let's look at an example of using these operators:

```
Observable<String> words = Observable // (1)
    .just("one", "way", "or", "another", "I'll", "learn", "RxJava")
    .zipWith(
      Observable.interval(200L, TimeUnit.MILLISECONDS),
      (x, y) -> x
    );
```

```
Observable<Long> interval = Observable
    .interval(500L, TimeUnit.MILLISECONDS);
subscribePrint(words.takeUntil(interval), "takeUntil"); // (2)
subscribePrint( // (3)
    words.takeWhile(word -> word.length() > 2), "takeWhile"
);
subscribePrint(words.skipUntil(interval), "skipUntil"); // (4)
```

Let's take a look at the following explanation:

1. For these examples, we'll use the *words* and *interval* Observable instances. The *words* Observable instance emits a word every 200 milliseconds, and the *interval* Observable emits every half a second.

2. As mentioned previously, this overload of the takeUntil() operator will emit words until the interval Observable emits. So, the words one and way will be emitted because the next word, or, should be emitted 600 milliseconds after the subscription, and the interval Observable emits on the 500th millisecond.

3. Here, the takeWhile() operator puts a condition on the words Observable. It will emit only while there are words that contain more than two letters. Because 'or' has two letters, it won't be emitted and all the words after it will be skipped too. The takeUntil() operator has a similar overload, but it emits only words containing fewer than three letters. There is no takeWhile(Observable) operator overload as it would be zip() operator essentially: emit only if the other emits too.

4. The skip* operators are analogous to the take* ones. The difference is that they don't emit until/while a condition is satisfied. In this example, the words one and way are skipped because they are emitted before the 500th millisecond of subscribing and the interval Observable begins emitting at the 500th millisecond. The word 'or' and all the words coming after it are emitted.

These *conditional* operators can be used, for example, for displaying loading animation in GUI applications. The code can be something like this:

```
loadingAnimationObservable.takeUntil(requestObservable);
```

On every emission of the loadingAnimationObservable variable, some short-lived animation will be displayed to the user. When the request is returned, the animation will no longer be displayed. This is another way of branching the logic of a program.

The defaultIfEmpty( ) operator

The idea of the `defaultIfEmpty()` operator is to return something useful if an unknown source turns out to be empty. For example, we'll use locally stored information, if a remote source has nothing new.

Here's a simple example:

```
Observable<Object> test = Observable
    .empty()
    .defaultIfEmpty(5);
subscribePrint(test, "defaultIfEmpty");
```

Of course, this will output 5 and will complete.

> The source code for the `amb()`, `take*`, `skip*`, and `defaultIfEmpty()` operator examples can be found at https://github.com/meddle0x53/learning-rxjava/blob/master/src/main/java/com/packtpub/reactive/chapter05/Conditionals.java.

Until now, we have transformed, filtered, and combined data. But what about the *errors*? Our applications can enter into error state at any time. Yes, we can subscribe for *errors* emitted by the `Observable` instances, but this will terminate our logic. In the `subscribe` method, we are outside of the `Observable` chain of operators. What if we want to react to an *error* from within the `Observable` instances chain and to try to prevent the termination? There are some operators that help us do that, and we'll be examining them in the next section.

Handling errors

When dealing with *errors* in RxJava, you should be aware that they terminate the `Observable` chain of actions. Much like with your normal procedural code, once you are in the catch block, you can't go back to the code that has thrown the exception. You can execute some backup logic though and use it instead of failing the program. The `return*`, `retry*`, and `resume*` operators do something similar.

The return and resume operators

The onErrorReturn operator can be used in order to prevent the Subscriber instance's onError from being called. Instead, it will emit one last item and complete. Here is an example:

```
Observable<String> numbers = Observable
    .just("1", "2", "three", "4", "5")
    .map(Integer::parseInt)
    .onErrorReturn(e -> -1);
    subscribePrint(numbers, "Error returned");
```

The Integer::parseInt method will succeed in converting the strings 1 and 2 to Integer values, but it will fail on three with a NumberFormatException exception. This exception will be passed to the onErrorReturn() method, which will return the number -1. The numbers Observable instance will emit the number -1 and complete. So the output will be 1, 2, -1, OnCompleted notification.

This is fine, but sometimes we'll want to switch to another Observable chain of operations on exception. For that, we can use the onExceptionResumeNext() operator, which returns a backup Observable instance that will replace the source one when an Exception occurs. Here is the code modified to use it:

```
Observable<Integer> defaultOnError =
    Observable.just(5, 4, 3, 2, 1);
Observable<String> numbers = Observable
    .just("1", "2", "three", "4", "5")
    .map(Integer::parseInt)
    .onExceptionResumeNext(defaultOnError);
    subscribePrint(numbers, "Exception resumed");
```

Now this will output 1, 2, 5, 4, 3, 2, 1, OnCompleted notification because, after the Exception raised on 'three', the defaultOnError Observable instance passed to onExceptionResumeNext() method will begin emitting, replacing the source Observable instance for all the Subscriber methods.

There is one other resuming() operator very similar to onExceptionResumeNext(). It is called onErrorResumeNext(). It can replace the onExceptionResumeNext() operator in the preceding example, and the result will be the same. There are two differences between these two operators though.

First, the `onErrorResumeNext()` operator has an additional overload that takes a lambda expression, returning the `Observable` instance (similar to the `onErrorReturn()` method). Second, it will react to every kind of error. The `onExceptionResumeNext()` method reacts only to instances of the `Exception` class and its subclasses.

```
Observable<String> numbers = Observable
    .just("1", "2", "three", "4", "5")
    .doOnNext(number -> {
      assert !number.equals("three");
    }
    .map(Integer::parseInt)
    .onErrorResumeNext(defaultOnError);
    subscribePrint(numbers, "Error resumed");
```

In this example, the result will be the same as in the preceding one (1, 2, 5, 4, 3, 2, 1, OnCompleted notification b); it doesn't matter that there is an *assertion error*. But if we've used an `onExceptionResumeNext()` operator, the error would have reached the `subscribePrint` method as an `OnError` *notification*.

The `doOnNext()` operator used in this example is a *side effect generator*. It doesn't change the items emitted by the `Observable` instance it is called upon. It can be used for logging, caching, asserting, or adding additional logic. There are `doOnError()` and `doOnCompleted()` operators too. In addition, there is a `finallyDo()` operator, which executes the function passed to it when there is an error or when the `Observable` instance has completed.

The retrying technique

Retrying is an important technique. When an `Observable` instance is emitting data from an uncertain source (for example, a remote server), one network problem could terminate the whole application. Retrying on *errors* saves us in situations like this.

Inserting the `retry()` operator into the `Observable` action chain means that if an *error* occurs, the subscribers will resubscribe to the source `Observable` instance and try everything from the beginning of the chain. If there is an *error* again, everything is restarted once more. The `retry()` operator without parameters retries infinitely. There is an overload `retry(int)` method, which takes the number of the maximum allowed retry attempts.

In order to demonstrate the `retry()` method, we will use the following special behavior:

```java
class FooException extends RuntimeException {
  public FooException() {
    super("Foo!");
  }
}

class BooException extends RuntimeException {
  public BooException() {
    super("Boo!");
  }
}
class ErrorEmitter implements OnSubscribe<Integer> {
  private int throwAnErrorCounter = 5;
  @Override
  public void call(Subscriber<? super Integer> subscriber) {
    subscriber.onNext(1);
    subscriber.onNext(2);
    if (throwAnErrorCounter > 4) {
      throwAnErrorCounter--;
      subscriber.onError(new FooException());
      return;
    }
    if (throwAnErrorCounter > 0) {
      throwAnErrorCounter--;
      subscriber.onError(new BooException());
      return;
    }
    subscriber.onNext(3);
    subscriber.onNext(4);
    subscriber.onCompleted();
    }
  }
}
```

An `ErrorEmitter` instance can be passed to the `Observable.create()` method. If the `throwAnErrorCounter` field is a number greater than four, a `FooException` exception is sent; if it's greater than zero, a `BooException` exception is sent, and if it's less than or equal to zero, it sends some events and completes normally.

Now let's look at this example of using the `retry()` operator:

```
subscribePrint(Observable.create(new ErrorEmitter()).retry(),
"Retry");
```

Because the initial value of the `throwAnErrorCounter` field is five, it will retry `five` times, and when the counter becomes zero, the `Observable` instance will *complete*. The result will be 1, 2, 1, 2, 1, 2, 1, 2, 1, 2, 1, 2, 3, 4, `OnCompleted` notification.

The `retry()` operator can be used to retry a set number of times (or indefinitely). It even has an overload, taking a function with two arguments—the number of the retries until now and cause `Throwable` instance. If this function returns `True`, the `Observable` instance is resubscribed to. This is a way of writing custom retry logic. But what about delayed retries? For example, retrying every second? There is one special operator capable of very complex *retrying logic*, the `retryWhen()` operator. Let's look at an example of using it and the previously mentioned `retry(predicate)` operator:

```
Observable<Integer> when = Observable.create(new ErrorEmitter())
    .retryWhen(attempts -> {
      return attempts.flatMap(error -> {
        if (error instanceof FooException) {
          System.err.println("Delaying...");
          return Observable.timer(1L, TimeUnit.SECONDS);
        }
        return Observable.error(error);
      });
    })
    .retry((attempts, error) -> {
      return (error instanceof BooException) && attempts < 3;
    });
subscribePrint(when, "retryWhen");
```

When the `retryWhen()` operator returns an `Observable` instance, emitting the `OnError()` or `OnCompleted()` notifications, the notification is propagated, and if there is no other *retry/resume*, the `onError()` or `onCompleted()` methods of the subscribers are called. Otherwise, the subscribers will be resubscribed to the source observable.

In this example, if the `Exception` is `FooException`, the `retryWhen()` operator returns an `Observable` instance emitting after a second. That's how we implement retrying with a delay. If the `Exception` is not `FooException`, it is propagated to the next `retry(predicate)` operator. It can check the type of the *error* and the number of attempts and decide if it should propagate the error or retry the source.

In this example, we'll get one delayed retry, three retries from the
`retry(predicate)` method, and on the fifth try, the subscribers will receive an
`OnError` notification, with a `BooException` exception.

 The source code for the `retry/resume/return` examples can
be found at `https://github.com/meddle0x53/learning-`
`rxjava/blob/master/src/main/java/com/packtpub/`
`reactive/chapter05/HandlingErrors.java`.

The last section of this chapter is saved for a more complex example. We'll use our
knowledge so far to create a request to remote HTTP API and handle the result,
outputting it to the user.

An HTTP client example

Let's use RxJava to retrieve information about the GitHub repositories of a user by
username. We will use our `subscribePrint()` function used previously to output
the information to the system output. The idea of the program is to display all of the
public repositories of the user that are not forks. The main part of the program looks
like this:

```
String username = "meddle0x53";
Observable<Map> resp = githubUserInfoRequest(client, username);
subscribePrint(
  resp
  .map(json ->
    json.get("name") + "(" + json.get("language") + ")"),
  "Json"
);
```

This program uses my user (it can be easily reworked to use a *username* passed as a
parameter) to retrieve information its public repositories. It prints the name of each
repository and the main programming language used in it. The repositories are
represented by `Map` instances generated from the incoming JSON file, so we can read
repository properties from them.

These JSON `Map` instances are emitted by an `Observable` instance, created by the
`githubUserInfoRequest(client, username)` method. The client parameter is an
instance of Apache's `HttpAsyncClient` class. The client is capable of performing
asynchronous HTTP requests, and there is an additional RxJava module, called
`RxApacheHttp`, that gives us bindings between RxJava and Apache HTTP. We'll be
using it for our HTTP request implementation; you can find it at `https://github.`
`com/ReactiveX/RxApacheHttp`.

There are many additional RxJava projects, placed at `https://github.com/ReactiveX`. Some of them are very useful. For example, most of the `from(Stream/Reader/File)` methods that we have implemented in this book have better implementations in the RxJavaString module.

The next step is to implement the `githubUserInfoRequest(HttpAsyncClient, String)` method:

```
Observable<Map> githubUserInfoRequest(HttpAsyncClient client,
String githubUser) {
  if (githubUser == null) { // (1)
    return Observable.<Map>error(
      new NullPointerException("Github user must not be null!")
    );
  }
  String url = "https://api.github.com/users/" + githubUser +
  "/repos";
  return requestJson(client, url) // (2)
  .filter(json -> json.containsKey("git_url")) // (3)
  .filter(json -> json.get("fork").equals(false));
}
```

This method is fairly simple too.

1. First we need to have a GitHub *username* in order to execute our request, so we do some checking for it. It should not be `null`. If it's `null`, we'll return an *error-emitting* `Observable` instance, emitting an `OnError` notification with a `NullPointerException` exception. Our printing subscriber function will display it to the users.

2. In order to do the actual HTTP request, we'll use another method with the signature `requestJson(HttpAsyncClient, String)`. It is the one returning the `Observable` instance, emitting JSON represented by the Map instances.

3. If the user is not a real GitHub user, or if we've exceeded the GitHub API limit, GitHub will send us a JSON message. That's why we need to check whether the JSON we've got contains repository data or something else. The JSON representing a repository has a `git_url` key. We use this to filter only JSONs that represent GitHub repositories.

4. We need only the non-fork repositories; that's why we filter them.

This is again quite simple to understand. Up until now, we've used only the `map()` and `filter()` operators in our logic, nothing special. Let's look at the actual HTTP request implementation:

```
Observable<Map> requestJson(HttpAsyncClient client, String url) {
  Observable<String> rawResponse = ObservableHttp
  .createGet(url, client)
  .toObservable() // (1)
  .flatMap(resp -> resp.getContent() // (2)
    .map(bytes -> new String(
      bytes,  java.nio.charset.StandardCharsets.UTF_8
    ))
  )
  .retry(5) // (3)
  .cast(String.class) // (4)
  .map(String::trim)
  .doOnNext(resp -> getCache(url).clear()); // (5)
```

1. The `ObservableHttp` class comes from the `RxApacheHttp` module. It does the asynchronous HTTP request for us, using the Apache `HttpClient` instance. The `createGet(url, client)` method returns an instance that can be converted into an actual `Observable` instance with the `toObservable()` method. We do exactly that here.

2. This `Observable` instance, when it receives the HTTP response, will emit it as an `ObservableHttpResponse` instance. This instance has a `getContent()` method, which returns an `Observable<byte[]>` object, representing the response as a *sequence of bytes*. We turn these *byte arrays* into `String` objects with a simple `map()` operator. Now we have a JSON response represented by a `String` object.

3. If there is some problem connecting to GitHub, we *retry* five times.

4. The cast to `String` is necessary because of Java's type system. Additionally, we remove any trailing/leading white spaces from the response, using the `trim()` method.

5. We clear the cached information for this URL. We use a simple in-memory Map instance from URL to JSON data cache implementation in order to not repeat the same request multiple times. How do we fill up this cache? We'll see soon in the following piece of code. Let's take a look at it:

```
// (6)
Observable<String> objects = rawResponse
  .filter(data -> data.startsWith("{"))
  .map(data -> "[" + data + "]");
```

```
Observable<String> arrays = rawResponse
  .filter(data -> data.startsWith("["));
Observable<Map> response = arrays
  .ambWith(objects) // (7)
  .map(data -> { // (8)
    return new Gson().fromJson(data, List.class);
  })
  .flatMapIterable(list -> list) // (9)
  .cast(Map.class)
  .doOnNext(json -> getCache(url).add(json)); // (10)
  return Observable.amb(fromCache(url), response); // (11)
}
```

6. The response can be either a JSON array or a JSON object; we branch our logic using the `filter()` operator here. The JSON object is turned to a JSON array in order to use common logic later.

7. Using the `ambWith()` operator, we'll use the one emitting data from the two `Observable` instances and treat the result as a JSON array. We will have either array or object JSON, and in the end, the result is just an `Observable` instance emitting a JSON array as a `String` object.

8. We turn this `String` object into actual List of Map instances, using Google's JSON library.

9. The `flatMapIterable()` operator flattens the `Observable` instance emitting a `List` instance to one that emits its contents — multiple Map instances representing JSON.

10. All of these Map instances are cached by adding them to the in-memory cache.

11. Using the `amb()` operator, we implement the fallback-to-cache mechanism. If the cache contains data, it will emit first, and this data will be used instead.

We have a real example of HTTP data retrieval, implemented using `Observable` instances! The output of this request look like this:

```
Json : of-presentation-14 (JavaScript)
Json : portable-vim (null)
Json : pro.js (JavaScript)
Json : tmangr (Ruby)
Json : todomvc-proact (JavaScript)
Json : vimconfig (VimL)
Json : vimify (Ruby)
Json ended!
```

The source code for the preceding example can be found at `https://github.com/meddle0x53/learning-rxjava/blob/master/src/main/java/com/packtpub/reactive/chapter05/HttpRequestsExample.java`.

Summary

In this chapter, we've learned how to combine `Observable` instances, how to create dependencies between them, and how to react to errors. As we've seen in the final example, we are now capable of creating quite complex logic using just `Observable` instances and their operators. Adding to that the RxJava modules available on the Internet, we can turn almost every data source into an `Observable` instance.

The next step is to master Schedulers. They will provide us with the power to handle multi-threading while coding using this reactive style of programming. Java is famous for its concurrency; it is time to add these capabilities of the language to our `Observable` chains, doing multiple HTTP requests in parallel (for example). Another new thing we'll learn is how to **buffer**, **throttle**, and **debounce** our data, techniques that come hand-in-hand with real-time data streams.

6
Using Concurrency and Parallelism with Schedulers

Modern processors have multiple cores and enable many time-consuming operations to be processed faster simultaneously. The Java concurrency API (which includes threads and much more) makes it possible to do just that.

RxJava's `Observable` chains seem a good match for the threads. It would be great if we could *subscribe* to our source and do all the transforming, combining, and filtering in the background and, when everything is done, have the result to be passed to the main threads. Yes, this sounds wonderful, but RxJava is single-threaded by default. This means that, in the most cases, when the `subscribe` method is called on an `Observable` instance, the current thread blocks until everything is emitted. (This is not true for the `Observable` instances created by the `interval` or `timer` factory methods, for example.). This is a good thing because working with threads is not so easy. They are powerful, but they need to be synchronized with each other; for example, when one depends on the result of another.

One of the hardest things to manage in a multi-threaded environment is the shared data between the threads. One thread could read from a data source while another is modifying it, which leads to different versions of the same data being used by the different threads. If an `Observable` chain is constructed the right way, there is no shared state. This means that synchronization is not so complex.

In this chapter, we will talk about executing things in parallel and look at what concurrency means. Additionally, we'll learn some techniques for handling the situation when too many items are emitted by our Observable instances (a situation which is not so rare in the multi-threaded environment). The topics covered in this chapter are as follows:

- Using Scheduler instances to achieve *concurrency*
- **Buffering, throttling,** and **debouncing** with Observable instances

RxJava's schedulers

The schedulers are the RxJava's way of achieving concurrency. They are in charge of creating and managing the threads for us (internally relying on Java's threadpool facilities). We won't be dealing with Java's concurrency API and its quirks and complexities. We've been using the schedulers all along, implicitly with timers and intervals, but the time has come to master them.

Let's recall the Observable.interval factory method, which we introduced back in *Chapter 3, Creating and Connecting Observables, Observers, and Subjects*. As we saw before, RxJava is *single-threaded* by *default*, so in most cases, calling the subscribe method on the Observable instance will block the current thread. But that is not the case with the interval Observable instances. If we look at the JavaDoc of the Observable<Long> interval(long interval, TimeUnit unit) method, we'll see that it says that the Observable instance created by it operates on something called '*the computation Scheduler*'.

In order to inspect the behavior of the interval method (as well as other things in this chapter) we will need a powerful debugging utility. That's why the first thing we'll be doing in this chapter is implementing it.

Debugging Observables and their schedulers

In the previous chapter, we've introduced the doOnNext() operator, which could be used for logging the emitted items directly from within the Observable chain. We mentioned that there are doOnError() and doOnCompleted() operators too. But there is one that combines all three of them—the doOnEach() operator. We can log everything from it because it receives all the notifications emitted, regardless of their type. We can put it halfway through the chain of operators and use it to log, say, the state there. It takes a Notification -> void function.

Here is the source of a higher order *debug* function returning a `lambda` result, which is capable of logging the emissions of an `Observable` instance labeled, using the passed description:

```
<T> Action1<Notification<? super T>> debug(
  String description, String offset
) {
  AtomicReference<String> nextOffset = new
  AtomicReference<String>(">");
  return (Notification<? super T> notification) -> {
    switch (notification.getKind()) {
    case OnNext:
      System.out.println(
        Thread.currentThread().getName() +
        "|" + description + ": " + offset +
        nextOffset.get() + notification.getValue()
      );
      break;
    case OnError:
      System.err.println(
        Thread.currentThread().getName() +
        "|" + description + ": " + offset +
        nextOffset.get() + " X " + notification.getThrowable()
      );
      break;
    case OnCompleted:
      System.out.println(
        Thread.currentThread().getName() +
        "|" + description + ": " + offset +
        nextOffset.get() + "|"
      );
    default:
      break;
    }
    nextOffset.getAndUpdate(p -> "-" + p);
  };
}
```

Depending on the passed *description* and *offset*, the returned method logs each notification. The important thing, however, is that it logs the current active thread's name before everything else. <value> marks the *OnNext notifications*; x, the *OnError notifications*; and |, the *OnCompleted notifications*, and the `nextOffset` variable is used to show the values in time.

Here is an example of using this new method:

```
Observable
    .range(5, 5)
    .doOnEach(debug("Test", ""))
    .subscribe();
```

This example will generate five sequential numbers, beginning with the number five. We pass a call to our `debug(String, String)` method to the `doOnEach()` operator to log everything after the call of the `range()` method. With a subscribe call without parameters, this little chain will be triggered. The output is as follows:

```
main|Test: >5

main|Test: ->6

main|Test: -->7

main|Test: --->8

main|Test: ---->9

main|Test: ----->|
```

The first thing logged is the name of the current thread (the main one), then we have the description of the `Observable` instance passed to the `debug()` method, and after that, a colon and dashes forming arrows, representing the time. Finally we have the symbol of the type of the notification — the value itself for values and | for completed.

Let's define one overload to the `debug()` helper method so that we don't need to pass a second parameter to it with an additional offset, if it is not needed:

```
<T> Action1<Notification<? super T>> debug(String description) {
    return debug(description, "");
}
```

The code for the preceding methods can be viewed/downloaded at: https://github.com/meddle0x53/learning-rxjava/blob/ master/src/main/java/com/packtpub/reactive/common/ Helpers.java.

Now we are ready to debug what's happening with the `Observable` instances, created by the interval method!

The interval Observable and its default scheduler

Let's examine the following example:

```
Observable
  .take(5)
  .interval(500L, TimeUnit.MILLISECONDS)
  .doOnEach(debug("Default interval"))
  .subscribe();
```

This creates an `interval` `Observable` instance, emitting every half second. We use the `take()` method to get only the first five *notifications* and to complete. We'll use our `debug()` helper method to log the values, emitted by the `Observable` instance, created by the interval method and use the call to `subscribe()`, which will trigger the logic. The output should look like this:

```
RxComputationThreadPool-1|Default interval: >0

RxComputationThreadPool-1|Default interval: ->1

RxComputationThreadPool-1|Default interval: -->2

RxComputationThreadPool-1|Default interval: --->3

RxComputationThreadPool-1|Default interval: ---->4
```

Everything should be familiar here, except the thread that the `Observable` instance executes on! This thread is not the *main* one. It seems it is created by a RxJava-managed pool of reusable `Thread` instances, judging by its name (`RxComputationThreadPool-1`).

If you recall, the `Observable.interval` factory method had the following overload:

```
Observable<Long> interval(long, TimeUnit, Scheduler)
```

This means that we can specify a scheduler on which it will operate. It was mentioned previously, that the overload with only two parameters operates on the *computation* scheduler. So, now let's try passing another scheduler and see what's going to happen:

```
Observable
  .take(5)
  .interval(500L, TimeUnit.MILLISECONDS, Schedulers.immediate())
  .doOnEach(debug("Imediate interval"))
  .subscribe();
```

This is the same as before, but with one little difference. We pass a scheduler called *immediate*. The idea is to execute the work immediately on the currently running thread. The result is as follows:

```
main|Imediate interval: >0
main|Imediate interval: ->1
main|Imediate interval: -->2
main|Imediate interval: --->3
main|Imediate interval: ---->4
```

By specifying this scheduler, we made the `interval` `Observable` instance run on the current, *main* thread.

 The source code for the preceding example can be found at `https://github.com/meddle0x53/learning-rxjava/blob/master/src/main/java/com/packtpub/reactive/chapter06/IntervalAndSchedulers.java`.

With the help of the schedulers, we can instruct our operators to run on a particular thread or to use a particular pool of threads.

Everything we just covered leads us to the conclusion that the schedulers spawn new threads, or reuse already spawned ones on which the *operations*, part of the `Observable` instance chain, execute. Thus, we can achieve concurrency (operators making progress at the same time) by using only them.

In order to have *multi-threaded* logic, we'll have to learn just these two things:

- The types of schedulers we can chose from
- How to use these schedulers with an arbitrary `Observable` chain of *operations*

Types of schedulers

There are several types of `schedulers` dedicated for certain kinds of actions. In order to learn more about them, let's take a look at the `Scheduler` class.

It turns out that the class is quite simple. It has only two methods, as follows:

- `long now()`
- `abstract Worker createWorker()`

The first one returns the current time in milliseconds, and the second creates a `Worker` instance. These `Worker` instances are used for executing actions on a single thread or event loop (depending on the implementation). Scheduling actions for execution is done using the Worker's `schedule*` methods. The `Worker` class implements the `Subscription` interface, so it has an `unsubscribe()` method. *Unsubscribing* the `Worker` *unschedules* all outstanding work and allows a resource cleanup.

We can use the workers to perform scheduling outside the `Observable` context. For every `Scheduler` type, we can do the following:

```
scheduler.createWorker().schedule(Action0);
```

This will schedule the passed action and execute it. In most cases, this method shouldn't be used directly for scheduling work, we just pick the right scheduler and schedule actions on it instead. In order to understand what they do, we can use the method to inspect the various types of schedulers available.

Let's define a testing method:

```
void schedule(Scheduler scheduler, int numberOfSubTasks,
boolean onTheSameWorker) {
  List<Integer> list = new ArrayList<>(0);
  AtomicInteger current = new AtomicInteger(0);
  Random random = new Random();
  Worker worker = scheduler.createWorker();
  Action0 addWork = () -> {
    synchronized (current) {
      System.out.println("  Add : " +
      Thread.currentThread().getName() + " " + current.get());
      list.add(random.nextInt(current.get()));
      System.out.println("  End add : " +
      Thread.currentThread().getName() + " " + current.get());
    }
  };
  Action0 removeWork = () -> {
    synchronized (current) {
      if (!list.isEmpty()) {
        System.out.println("  Remove : " +
        Thread.currentThread().getName());
        list.remove(0);
        System.out.println("  End remove : " +
        Thread.currentThread().getName());
      }
    }
  };
```

```
Action0 work = () -> {
  System.out.println(Thread.currentThread().getName());
  for (int i = 1; i <= numberOfSubTasks; i++) {
    current.set(i);
    System.out.println("Begin add!");
    if (onTheSameWorker) {
      worker.schedule(addWork);
    }
    else {
      scheduler.createWorker().schedule(addWork);
    }
    System.out.println("End add!");
  }
  while (!list.isEmpty()) {
    System.out.println("Begin remove!");
    if (onTheSameWorker) {
      worker.schedule(removeWork);
    }
    else {
      scheduler.createWorker().schedule(removeWork);
    }
    System.out.println("End remove!");
  };
  worker.schedule(work);
}
```

The method uses the passed Scheduler instance to do some work. There is an option to specify whether it should use the same Worker instance for every task, or spawn a new one for every sub-task. Basically, the dummy work consists of filling up a list with random numbers and then removing these numbers one by one. Every *add operation* and *remove operation* are scheduled via the worker created by the passed Scheduler instance as a sub-task. And before and after every sub-task the current thread and some additional information is logged.

> In a real-world scenario, once all the work has been done, we should always invoke the worker.unsubscribe() method.

Turning to the predefined Scheduler instances. They can be retrieved via a set of static methods contained in the Schedulers class. We will be using the debugging method defined previously to inspect their behavior in order to learn their differences and usefulness.

The Schedulers.immediate scheduler

The `Schedulers.immediate` scheduler executes work here and now. When an action is passed to its worker's `schedule(Action0)` method, it is just called. Let's suppose we run our test method with it, like this:

```
schedule(Schedulers.immediate(), 2, false);
schedule(Schedulers.immediate(), 2, true);
```

In both the cases, the result will look like this:

```
main
Begin add!
  Add : main 1
  End add : main 1
End add!
Begin add!
  Add : main 2
  End add : main 2
End add!
Begin remove!
  Remove : main
  End remove : main
End remove!
Begin remove!
  Remove : main
  End remove : main
End remove!
```

In other words, everything is executed on the caller thread—the main one and nothing is in parallel.

This scheduler can be used to execute methods, such as `interval()` and `timer()`, in the foreground.

The Schedulers.trampoline scheduler

The scheduler, retrieved by the `Schedulers.trampoline` method *enqueues* sub-tasks on the current `thread`. The enqueued work is executed after the work currently in progress completes. Say we were to run this:

```
schedule(Schedulers.trampoline(), 2, false);
schedule(Schedulers.trampoline(), 2, true);
```

In the first case, the result will be the same as with the immediate scheduler, because all the tasks are executed in their own `Worker` instances and, therefore, there is only one task to be enqueued for execution in every worker. But when we use the same `Worker` instance for scheduling every sub-task, we get this:

```
main
Begin add!
End add!
Begin add!
End add!
  Add : main 2
  End add : main 2
  Add : main 2
  End add : main 2
```

In other words, it will first execute the entire main action and after that, the sub-tasks; thus, the `List` instance will be filled in (the sub-tasks were enqueued) but never emptied. That's because, while executing the main task, the `List` instance was still empty and the `while` loop was not triggered.

The *trampoline* scheduler is useful for avoiding a `StackOverflowError` exception while running many tasks recursively. For example, let's assume a task completes and then calls itself to perform some new work. In the case of a single-threaded environment, this would lead to stack overflow due to the recursion; however, if we use the *trampoline* scheduler, it will serialize all scheduled activities and the stack depth will remain normal. However, the *trampoline* scheduler is usually slower than the *immediate* one. So, using the correct one depends on the use case.

The Schedulers.newThread scheduler

This schedule creates a *new* Thread instance (a single-threaded ScheduledThreadPoolExecutor instance to be precise) for every new Worker instance. Additionally, each worker enqueues the actions it receives through its schedule() method, much like the trampoline scheduler does. Let's look at the following code:

```
schedule(Schedulers.newThread(), 2, true);
```

It will have the same behavior as the *trampoline* but it will run in a new thread:

```
RxNewThreadScheduler-1
Begin add!
End add!
Begin add!
End add!
  Add : RxNewThreadScheduler-1 2
  End add : RxNewThreadScheduler-1 2
  Add : RxNewThreadScheduler-1 2
  End add : RxNewThreadScheduler-1 2
```

Instead, if we call the testing method like this:

```
schedule(Schedulers.newThread(), 2, false);
```

This will spawn a new Thread instance for every *sub-task*, which will produce output similar to this:

```
RxNewThreadScheduler-1
Begin add!
End add!
Begin add!
  Add : RxNewThreadScheduler-2 1
  End add : RxNewThreadScheduler-2 2
End add!
Begin remove!
  Add : RxNewThreadScheduler-3 2
  End add : RxNewThreadScheduler-3 2
End remove!
Begin remove!
End remove!
Begin remove!
```

```
    Remove : RxNewThreadScheduler-5
    End remove : RxNewThreadScheduler-5
    Remove : RxNewThreadScheduler-4
    End remove : RxNewThreadScheduler-4
End remove!
```

By using the *new thread* Scheduler instance, you can execute background tasks.

 A very important requirement here is that its workers need to be *unsubscribed* to avoid leaking threads and OS resources. Note that it is expensive to create new threads each time, so in most cases, the *computation* and the *IO* Scheduler instances should be used.

The Schedulers.computation scheduler

The computation scheduler is very similar to the *new thread* one, but it takes into account the number of processors/cores that the machine on which it runs has, and uses a thread pool that can reuse a limited number of threads. Every new Worker instance schedules sequential actions on one of these Thread instances. If the thread is not used at the moment they are executed, and if it is active, they are enqueued to execute on it later.

If we use the same Worker instance, we'll just enqueue all the actions on its thread and the result will be the same as scheduling with one Worker instance, using the *new thread* Scheduler instance.

My machine has four cores. Say I call the testing method on it like this:

```
schedule(Schedulers.computation(), 5, false);
```

I'd get output similar to this:

```
RxComputationThreadPool-1
Begin add!
  Add : RxComputationThreadPool-2 1
  End add : RxComputationThreadPool-2 1
End add!
Begin add!
End add!
Begin add!
  Add : RxComputationThreadPool-3 3
  End add : RxComputationThreadPool-3 3
End add!
Begin add!
```

```
   Add : RxComputationThreadPool-4 4
End add!
Begin add!
   End add : RxComputationThreadPool-4 4
End add!
Begin remove!
End remove!
Begin remove!
   Add : RxComputationThreadPool-2 5
   End add : RxComputationThreadPool-2 5
End remove!
Begin remove!
End remove!
Begin remove!
End remove!
Begin remove!
End remove!
Begin remove!
End remove!
Begin remove!
End remove!
Begin remove!
   Remove : RxComputationThreadPool-3
End remove!
Begin remove!
   End remove : RxComputationThreadPool-3
   Remove : RxComputationThreadPool-2
End remove!
Begin remove!
   End remove : RxComputationThreadPool-2
End remove!
Begin remove!
   Remove : RxComputationThreadPool-2
End remove!
Begin remove!
End remove!
Begin remove!
End remove!
Begin remove!
End remove!
Begin remove!
   End remove : RxComputationThreadPool-2
```

```
   End remove!
     Remove : RxComputationThreadPool-2
   Begin remove!
     End remove : RxComputationThreadPool-2
   End remove!
     Add : RxComputationThreadPool-1 5
     End add : RxComputationThreadPool-1 5
     Remove : RxComputationThreadPool-1
     End remove : RxComputationThreadPool-1
```

Everything is executed using only four `Thread` instances from a pool (note that there is a way to limit the number of `Thread` instances to be less than the available processor count).

The *computation* `Scheduler` instance is your real choice for doing background work—computations or processing thus its name. You can use it for everything that should run in the background and is not an *IO* related or blocking operation.

The Schedulers.io scheduler

The Input-Output (IO) scheduler uses a `ScheduledExecutorService` instance to retrieve the threads from a *thread pool* for its workers. Unused threads are cached and reused on demand. It can spawn an arbitrary number of threads if it is necessary.

Again, if we run our example with only one `Worker` instance, the actions will be enqueued on its thread, and it will behave like the *computation* and *new thread* schedulers.

Say we run it with multiple `Worker` instances, like this:

```
   schedule(Schedulers.io(), 2, false);
```

It would produce `Thread` instances on demand from its *pool*. The result looks like this:

RxCachedThreadScheduler-1

Begin add!

End add!

Begin add!

  Add : RxCachedThreadScheduler-2 2

  End add : RxCachedThreadScheduler-2 2

End add!

Begin remove!

  Add : RxCachedThreadScheduler-3 2

```
   End add : RxCachedThreadScheduler-3 2
End remove!
Begin remove!
   Remove : RxCachedThreadScheduler-4
   End remove : RxCachedThreadScheduler-4
End remove!
Begin remove!
End remove!
Begin remove!
   Remove : RxCachedThreadScheduler-6
   End remove : RxCachedThreadScheduler-6
End remove!
```

The *IO* scheduler is reserved for blocking *IO operations*. Use it for requests to servers, reading from files and sockets, and other similar blocking tasks. Note that its thread pool is unbounded; if its workers are not unsubscribed, the pool will grow indefinitely.

> The source code for all the preceding code is located at `https://github.com/meddle0x53/learning-rxjava/blob/master/src/main/java/com/packtpub/reactive/chapter06/SchedulersTypes.java`.

The Schedulers.from(Executor) method

This can be used to create a custom `Scheduler` instance. If none of the predefined schedulers work for you, use this method, passing it to a `java.util.concurrent.Executor` instance, to implement the behavior you need.

Now that we've learned about how and when the predefined `Scheduler` instances should be used, is time to see how to integrate them with our `Observable` sequence.

Combining Observables and schedulers

In order to execute our observable logic on other threads, we can use the schedulers. There are two special operators, which receive `Scheduler` as a parameter and produce `Observable` instances, capable of performing operations on `Thread` instances different from the current one.

The Observable<T> subscribeOn(Scheduler) method

The `subscribeOn()` method creates an `Observable` instance, whose `subscribe` method causes the subscription to occur on a thread retrieved from the passed scheduler. For example, we have this:

```
Observable<Integer> range = Observable
    .range(20, 4)
    .doOnEach(debug("Source"));
range.subscribe();


System.out.println("Hey!");
```

We'll get this output:

```
main|Source:  >20
main|Source:  ->21
main|Source:  -->22
main|Source:  --->23
main|Source:  -------->|
Hey!
```

This is normal; calling the `subscribe` method executes the observable logic on the main thread, and only after all this is done, we see `'Hey!'`.

Let's modify the code to look like this:

```
CountDownLatch latch = new CountDownLatch(1);
Observable<Integer> range = Observable
    .range(20, 4)
    .doOnEach(debug("Source"))
    .subscribeOn(Schedulers.computation())
    .finallyDo(() -> latch.countDown());
range.subscribe();
System.out.println("Hey!");
latch.await();
```

The output changes to the following:

```
Hey!
RxComputationThreadPool-1|Source:  >20
```

```
RxComputationThreadPool-1|Source: ->21
RxComputationThreadPool-1|Source: -->22
RxComputationThreadPool-1|Source: --->23
RxComputationThreadPool-1|Source:--------->|
```

This means that the *caller* thread doesn't block printing 'Hey!' first or in between the the numbers, and all the `Observable` instance observable logic is executed on a *computation* thread. This way, you can use every scheduler you like to decide where to execute the work.

Here we need to mention something important about the `subscribeOn()` method. If you call it multiple times throughout the chain like this:

```
CountDownLatch latch = new CountDownLatch(1);
Observable<Integer> range = Observable
    .range(20, 3)
    .doOnEach(debug("Source"))
    .subscribeOn(Schedulers.computation());
Observable<Character> chars = range
    .map(n -> n + 48)
    .map(n -> Character.toChars(n))
    .subscribeOn(Schedulers.io())
    .map(c -> c[0])
    .subscribeOn(Schedulers.newThread())
    .doOnEach(debug("Chars ", "    "))
    .finallyDo(() -> latch.countDown());
chars.subscribe();
latch.await();
```

The call to it that is *the closest* to the beginning of the chain matters. Here we *subscribe* on the *computation* scheduler first, then on the *IO* scheduler, and then on the *new thread* scheduler, but our code will be executed on the *computation* scheduler because this is specified *first* in the chain.

```
RxComputationThreadPool-1|Source: >20
RxComputationThreadPool-1|Chars :      >D
RxComputationThreadPool-1|Source: ->21
RxComputationThreadPool-1|Chars :      ->E
RxComputationThreadPool-1|Source: -->22
RxComputationThreadPool-1|Chars :      -->F
RxComputationThreadPool-1|Source: --->|
RxComputationThreadPool-1|Chars :      --->|
```

In conclusion, don't specify a scheduler in methods producing `Observable` instances; leave this choice to the callers of your methods. Alternatively, make your methods receive a `Scheduler` instance as a parameter; like the `Observable.interval` method, for example.

> The `subscribeOn()` operator is usable with `Observable` instances that block the caller thread when one subscribes to them. Using the `subscribeOn()` method with such sources lets the caller thread progress concurrently with the `Observable` instance logic.

And what about the other operator, which helps us doing work on other threads?

The Observable<T> observeOn(Scheduler) operator

The `observeOn()` operator is similar to the `subscribeOn()` operator, but instead of executing the entire chain on the passed `Scheduler` instances, it executes the part of the chain from its place within it, onwards. The easiest way to understand this is through an example. Let's use the previous one, after slightly modifying it:

```
CountDownLatch latch = new CountDownLatch(1);
Observable<Integer> range = Observable
    .range(20, 3)
    .doOnEach(debug("Source"));
Observable<Character> chars = range
    .map(n -> n + 48)
    .doOnEach(debug("+48 ", "       "))
    .map(n -> Character.toChars(n))
    .map(c -> c[0])
    .observeOn(Schedulers.computation())
    .doOnEach(debug("Chars ", "       "))
    .finallyDo(() -> latch.countDown());
chars.subscribe();
System.out.println("Hey!");
latch.await();
```

Here, we tell the `Observable` chain to execute on the *main* thread after subscribing until it reaches the `observeOn()` operator. At this point, it is moved on the *computation* scheduler. The output of this is something similar to the following:

```
main|Source: >20
main|+48 :        >68
```

```
main|Source:  ->21
main|+48 :       ->69
main|Source:  -->22
main|+48 :       -->70
RxComputationThreadPool-3|Chars :       >D
RxComputationThreadPool-3|Chars :       ->E
RxComputationThreadPool-3|Chars :       -->F
main|Source:  --->|
main|+48 :       --->|
Hey!
RxComputationThreadPool-3|Chars :       --->|
```

As we can see, the part of the chain before the call to the operator blocks the *main* thread, preventing printing `Hey!`. However, after all the notifications pass through the `observeOn()` operator, `'Hey!'` is printed and the execution continues on the *computation* thread.

If we move the `observeOn()` operator up the `Observable` chain, a greater part of the logic will be executed using the *computation* scheduler.

Of course, the `observeOn()` operator can be used together with the `subscribeOn()` operator. That way, part of the chain could be executed on one thread and the rest of it on another (in most cases). This is especially useful if you code a client-side application because, normally, these applications run on one *event enqueueing* thread. You can read from files/servers using the *IO* scheduler with `subscribeOn()`/ `observeOn()` operator and then observe the result on the *event* thread.

> There is an Android module for RxJava that is not covered by this book, but it is getting quite a lot of attention. You can read more about it here: `https://github.com/ReactiveX/RxJava/wiki/The-RxJava-Android-Module`.
>
> If you are an Android developer don't miss it!
>
> There are similar modules for **Swing** and **JavaFx** as well.

Let's look at an example using both the `subscribeOn()` and `observeOn()` operators:

```
CountDownLatch latch = new CountDownLatch(1);
Observable<Integer> range = Observable
  .range(20, 3)
  .subscribeOn(Schedulers.newThread())
```

```
    .doOnEach(debug("Source"));
  Observable<Character> chars = range
    .observeOn(Schedulers.io())
    .map(n -> n + 48)
    .doOnEach(debug("+48 ",  "     "))
    .observeOn(Schedulers.computation())
    .map(n -> Character.toChars(n))
    .map(c -> c[0])
    .doOnEach(debug("Chars ",  "     "))
    .finallyDo(() -> latch.countDown());
  chars.subscribe();
  latch.await();
```

Here, we use one call for the `subsribeOn()` operator at the beginning of the chain (actually, it doesn't matter where we put it, because it is a sole call to that operator) and two calls for the `observeOn()` operator. The result of executing this code looks like this:

```
RxNewThreadScheduler-1|Source: >20

RxNewThreadScheduler-1|Source: ->21

RxNewThreadScheduler-1|Source: -->22

RxNewThreadScheduler-1|Source: --->|

RxCachedThreadScheduler-1|+48 :       >68

RxCachedThreadScheduler-1|+48 :       ->69

RxCachedThreadScheduler-1|+48 :       -->70

RxComputationThreadPool-3|Chars :     >D

RxCachedThreadScheduler-1|+48 :       --->|

RxComputationThreadPool-3|Chars :     ->E

RxComputationThreadPool-3|Chars :     -->F

RxComputationThreadPool-3|Chars :     --->|
```

We can see that the chain passes through three threads. If we do this with more elements, some of the code will be executed seemingly in *parallel*. The conclusion is that, using the `observeOn()` operator, we can change the threads multiple times; using the `subscribeOn()` operator, we can do this one time — *on subscription*.

> The source for the preceding examples with the `observeOn()`/ `subscribeOn()` operators can be found at https://github.com/meddle0x53/learning-rxjava/blob/master/src/main/java/com/packtpub/reactive/chapter06/SubscribeOnAndObserveOn.java.

With these two operators, we can have `Observable` instances and *multi-threading* working together. But being *concurrent* doesn't really mean that we can do things in *parallel*. It means that our program has multiple threads, making some progress independently. True parallelism is when our program uses the CPU (cores) of the machine it runs on at their maximum and its threads run literally at the same time.

All of our examples up until now just moved the chain logic onto another threads. Although, some of the examples really did part of their operations in *parallel*, but a true *parallelism* example looks different.

Parallelism

We can achieve *parallelism* only by using the operators that we already know. Think about the `flatMap()` operator; it creates an `Observable` instance for each item emitted by the source. If we call the `subscribeOn()` operator with a `Scheduler` instance on these `Observable` instances, each one of them will be *scheduled* on a new `Worker` instance, and they'll work in *parallel* (if the host machine allows that). Here is an example of this:

```
Observable<Integer> range = Observable
    .range(20, 5)
    .flatMap(n -> Observable
      .range(n, 3)
      .subscribeOn(Schedulers.computation())
      .doOnEach(debug("Source"))
    );
range.subscribe();
```

The output of this code looks like this:

```
RxComputationThreadPool-3|Source: >23
RxComputationThreadPool-4|Source: >20
RxComputationThreadPool-2|Source: >22
RxComputationThreadPool-3|Source: ->24
RxComputationThreadPool-1|Source: >21
RxComputationThreadPool-2|Source: ->23
RxComputationThreadPool-3|Source: -->25
RxComputationThreadPool-3|Source: --->|
RxComputationThreadPool-4|Source: ->21
RxComputationThreadPool-4|Source: -->22
RxComputationThreadPool-4|Source: --->|
```

```
RxComputationThreadPool-2|Source:  -->24
RxComputationThreadPool-2|Source:  --->|
RxComputationThreadPool-1|Source:  ->22
RxComputationThreadPool-1|Source:  -->23
RxComputationThreadPool-1|Source:  --->|
RxComputationThreadPool-4|Source:  >24
RxComputationThreadPool-4|Source:  ->25
RxComputationThreadPool-4|Source:  -->26
RxComputationThreadPool-4|Source:  --->|
```

We can see by the names of the threads that the `Observable` instances defined through the `flatMap()` operator are executed in *parallel*. And that's really the case — the four threads are using the four cores of my processor.

I'll provide another example, this time for *parallel* requests to a remote server. We'll be using the `requestJson()` method we defined in the previous chapter. The idea is this:

1. We'll retrieve information about the followers of a GitHub user (for this example we'll be using my account).
2. For every follower, we'll get the URL to its profile.
3. We will request the profiles of the followers in *parallel*.
4. We'll print the number of the followers and the number of their followers.

Let's see how this is implemented:

```
Observable<Map> response = CreateObservable.requestJson(
    client,
    "https://api.github.com/users/meddle0x53/followers"
); // (1)
response
    .map(followerJson -> followerJson.get("url")) // (2)
    .cast(String.class)
    .flatMap(profileUrl -> CreateObservable
      .requestJson(client, profileUrl)
      .subscribeOn(Schedulers.io()) // (3)
      .filter(res -> res.containsKey("followers"))
      .map(json ->  // (4)
        json.get("login") +  " : " +
        json.get("followers"))
    )
```

```
.doOnNext(follower -> System.out.println(follower)) // (5)
.count() // (6)
.subscribe(sum -> System.out.println("meddle0x53 : " + sum));
```

Here's what's happening in the preceding code:

1. First we perform a request to the followers data of my user.

2. The request returns the followers as *JSON* strings, which are converted into Map objects (see the implementation of the requestJson method). From each of the *JSON* files, the URL to the profile of the follower it represents is read.

3. A new request is executed for each of these URLs. The requests run in *parallel* on *IO* threads, because we use the same technique as in the previous example. It is worth mentioning that the flatMap() operator has an overload that takes a maxConcurrent integer parameter. We can limit the concurrent requests using it.

4. After user data for a follower is fetched, the information for his/her followers is generated.

5. This information is printed as a side effect.

6. We count my followers using the count() operator (which is the same as the scan(0.0, (sum, element) -> sum + 1).last() call). Then we print them. The order of the printed data is not guaranteed to be the same as the order in which the followers were traversed.

The source code for the preceding example can be found at https:// github.com/meddle0x53/learning-rxjava/blob/master/ src/main/java/com/packtpub/reactive/chapter06/ ParallelRequestsExample.java.

That's all about *concurrency* and *parallelism*. Everything is pretty simple, but powerful. There are a few rules (such as using the Subscribers.io instance for blocking operations, using the *computation* one for background tasks, and so on) that you must follow to ensure nothing goes wrong, even with *multi-threaded* observable chains of actions.

It is very possible using this *parallelism* technique to flood the Observable instance chain with data, and that's a problem. That's why we'll have to deal with it. Through the rest of this chapter, we'll learn how to handle too many elements coming from an *upstream* observable chains of actionse.

Buffering, throttling, and debouncing

Here is one interesting example:

```
Path path = Paths.get("src", "main", "resources");
Observable<String> data = CreateObservable
  .listFolder(path, "*")
  .flatMap(file -> {
    if (!Files.isDirectory(file)) {
      return CreateObservable
    .from(file)
    .subscribeOn(Schedulers.io());
  }
  return Observable.empty();
});
subscribePrint(data, "Too many lines");
```

This goes through all the files in a folder and reads all of them in parallel if they are not folders themselves. For the example, while I'm running it, there are five text files in the folder, and one of them is quite large. While printing the content of these files with our `subscribePrint()` method, we get something that looks like this:

Too many lines : Morbi nec nulla ipsum.

Too many lines : Proin eu tellus tortor.

Too many lines : Lorem ipsum dolor sit am

Error from Too many lines:

rx.exceptions.MissingBackpressureException

Too many lines : Vivamus non vulputate tellus, at faucibus nunc.

Too many lines : Ut tristique, orci eu

Too many lines : Aliquam egestas malesuada mi vitae semper.

Too many lines : Nam vitae consectetur risus, vitae congue risus.

Too many lines : Donec facilisis sollicitudin est non molestie.

   rx.internal.util.RxRingBuffer.onNext(RxRingBuffer.java:349)

   rx.internal.operators.OperatorMerge$InnerSubscriber.enqueue
   (OperatorMerge.java:721)

   rx.internal.operators.OperatorMerge$InnerSubscriber.emit
   (OperatorMerge.java:698)

   rx.internal.operators.OperatorMerge$InnerSubscriber.onNext
   (OperatorMerge.java:586)

   rx.internal.operators.OperatorSubscribeOn$1$1$1.onNext
   (OperatorSubscribeOn.java:76)

The output is cropped, but the important thing is that we get this `MissingBackpressureException` exception.

The threads reading each of the files are trying to push their data into the `merge()` operator (the `flatMap()` operator is implemented as `merge(map(func))`). The operator is struggling with a large amount of data, so it will try to notify the overproducing `Observable` instances to slow down (this ability to notify the upstream that the amount of data can't be handled is called *backpressure*). The problem is that they don't implement such a mechanism (*backpressure*), so the `MissingBackpressureException` exception is encountered.

Dealing with such a situation is achieved through implementing *backpressure* into the upstream observables, using one of the special `onBackpressure*` methods or by trying to avoid it by packaging the large amount of incoming items into a smaller set of emissions. This packaging is done through *buffering*, *dropping* some of the incoming items, *throttling* (buffering using time intervals or events), and *debouncing* (buffering using the intervals between emissions of items).

Let's examine some of them.

Throttling

Using this mechanism, we can regulate the emission rate of an `Observable` instance. We can specify time intervals or another flow-controlling `Observable` instance to achieve this.

Using the `sample()` operator, we can control the emissions of an `Observable` instance using another one, or a time interval.

```
data = data
  .sample(
    Observable
      .interval(100L, TimeUnit.MILLISECONDS)
      .take(10)
      .concatWith(
        Observable
          .interval(200L, TimeUnit.MILLISECONDS)
      )
  );
subscribePrint(data, "Too many lines");
```

The *sampling* Observable instance emits every 100 milliseconds for the first two seconds and then begins emitting every 200 milliseconds. The *data* Observable instance drops all of its items until the *sampling* emits. When this happens, the last item emitted by the *data* Observable instance is passed through. So we have great data loss, but it's harder to encounter the MissingBackpressureException exception (it is possible to get it, though).

The sample() operator has two additional overloads to which you can pass time intervals, a TimeUnit metric and, optionally, a Scheduler instance:

```
data = data.sample(
  100L,
  TimeUnit.MILLISECONDS
);
```

Using the sample() operator with the Observable instance gives us more detailed control over the data flow. The throttleLast() operator is just an alias for the different versions of the sample() operator that receive the time interval. The throttleFirst() operator is the same as the throttleLast() operator, but the *source* Observable instance will emit the first item it emitted at the beginning of the interval, instead of the last. These operators are running on the *computation* scheduler by default.

These techniques are useful (as well as most of the others in this section) when you have multiple, similar events. For example, if you want to capture and react to *mouse-move events*, you don't need all the events, containing all the pixel positions; you need only some of them.

Debouncing

In our previous example, *debouncing* won't work. Its idea is to emit only items that are not followed by other items for a given time interval. Therefore, some time must pass between emissions in order to propagate something. Because all of the items in our *data* Observable instances are emitted seemingly at once, there is no interval between them to use. So we need to change the example a bit in order to demonstrate this.

```
Observable<Object> sampler = Observable.create(subscriber -> {
  try {
    subscriber.onNext(0);
    Thread.sleep(100L);
    subscriber.onNext(10);
    Thread.sleep(200L);
    subscriber.onNext(20);
    Thread.sleep(150L);
```

```
    subscriber.onCompleted();
  }
  catch (Exception e) {
    subscriber.onError(e);
  }
}).repeat()
  .subscribeOn(Schedulers.computation());
data = data
  .sample(sampler)
  .debounce(150L, TimeUnit.MILLISECONDS);
```

Here we are using the `sample()` operator with a special *sampling* `Observable` instance in order to reduce the emissions to occur on 100, 200, and 150 milliseconds. By using the `repeat()` operator, we create an *infinite* `Observable` instance, repeating the source, and set it to execute on the *computation* scheduler. Now we can use the `debounce()` operator to emit only this set of items with time gaps between their emissions of 150 or more milliseconds.

Debouncing, like *throttling*, can be used to filter similar events from an over-producing source. A good example of this is an auto-complete search. We don't want to trigger searches on every letter inputted by the user; we need to wait for him/her to stop typing and then trigger the search. We can use the `debounce()` operator for that and set a reasonable *time interval*. The `debounce()` operator has an overload that takes a `Scheduler` instance as its third argument. Additionally, there is one more overload with a selector returning an `Observable` instance for more fine-grained control over the *data flow*.

The buffer and window operators

These two sets of operators are *transforming* operators much like the `map()` or `flatMap()` operators. They *transform* a series of elements in a collection—a sequence of these elements to be emitted as one.

This book will not cover these operators in detail, but it's worth mentioning that the `buffer()` operator has overloads that are able to collect emissions based on *time intervals*, *selectors*, and other `Observable` instances. It can be configured to skip items too. Here is an example with the `buffer(int count, int skip)` method, a version of the `buffer()` operator that collects *count* items and skips *skip* items:

```
data = data.buffer(2, 3000);
Helpers.subscribePrint(data, "Too many lines");
```

This will output something similar to the following:

```
Too many lines : ["Lorem ipsum dolor sit amet, consectetur adipiscing
elit.", "Donec facilisis sollicitudin est non molestie."]

Too many lines : ["Integer nec magna ac ex rhoncus imperdiet.",
"Nullam pharetra iaculis sem."]

Too many lines : ["Integer nec magna ac ex rhoncus imperdiet.",
"Nullam pharetra iaculis sem."]

Too many lines : ["Nam vitae consectetur risus, vitae congue risus.",
"Donec facilisis sollicitudin est non molestie."]

Too many lines : ["Sed mollis facilisis rutrum.", "Proin enim risus,
congue id eros at, pharetra consectetur ex."]

Too many lines ended!
```

The `window()` operator has exactly the same set of overloads as the `buffer()` operator. The difference is that instead of arrays of the buffered elements, the `Observable` instance created by the `window()` operator emits `Observable` instances emitting the collected elements.

In order to demonstrate a different overload, we'll present an example using the `window(long timespan, long timeshift, TimeUnit units)` method. This operator collects elements emitted within the *timespan* interval and skips all the elements emitted within the *timeshift* interval. This is repeated until the source `Observable` instance is complete.

```
data = data
    .window(3L, 200L, TimeUnit.MILLISECONDS)
    .flatMap(o -> o);
subscribePrint(data, "Too many lines");
```

We use the `flatMap()` operator to flatten the `Observable` instances. The result consists of all the items emitted in the first three milliseconds of the *subscription*, plus the ones emitted for three milliseconds after a 200-millisecond gap, and this is repeated while the source is emitting.

All the examples introduced in the preceding section can be found at https://github.com/meddle0x53/learning-rxjava/ blob/master/src/main/java/com/packtpub/reactive/ chapter06/BackpressureExamples.java.

The backpressure operators

The last set of operators preventing the `MissingBackpressureException` exception actually activate automatically when there is an overproducing *source* `Observable` instance.

The `onBackpressureBuffer()` operator buffers the items emitted by the faster than its `Observer` instance's *source* `Observable`. The buffered items are then emitted in a way that the subscribers can handle them. For example:

```
Helpers.subscribePrint(
  data.onBackpressureBuffer(10000),
  "onBackpressureBuffer(int)"
);
```

Here we used a big capacity for the buffer because of the large number of elements, but note that overflowing this buffer will get the `MissingBackpressureException` exception back.

The `onBackpressureDrop()` operator drops all the incoming items from the *source* `Observable` instance that can not be handled by the subscribers.

There is a way to establish *backpressure* by implementing smart Observables or Subscribers, but this topic is beyond the scope of this book. There is an excellent article about *backpressure* and observables on the RxJava wiki page—https:// github.com/ReactiveX/RxJava/wiki/Backpressure. Many of the operators mentioned in this section are described there in depth, and there are marble diagrams available to help you understand the more complex ones.

Summary

In this chapter, we've learned how to execute our observable logic on other threads that are different from the *main* one. There are some simple rules and techniques for doing this, and if everything is followed accordingly, there should be no dangers. Using these techniques, we are able to write *concurrent* programs. We've also learned how to achieve *parallel* execution using the schedulers and the `flatMap()` operator, and we saw a real-world example of doing that.

Another useful thing that we've examined was how to handle *overproducing* sources of data. There are a lot of operators that are able to do that by different means, and we introduced some of them, and talked about their usefulness.

With that, we have the knowledge to write arbitrary RxJava programs capable of working with data from different sources. We know how to do this using multiple threads. Using RxJava, its operators, and *constructions* is almost like coding using a new language. It has its rules and flow control methods.

In order to write stable applications, we'll have to learn how to *unit test* them. Testing *asynchronous* code is not an easy task. The good news is that there are some operators and classes provided by RxJava that are going to help us do that. You can read more about them in the next chapter.

7
Testing Your RxJava Application

While writing software, especially software which will be used by a lot of users, we need to be sure that everything is working correctly. We can write readable, well-structured, and modular code, which will make it easier for changing and maintaining. We should write tests because, with every feature, there is the danger of regression. When we already have tests for the existing code, refactoring it won't be as hard, because the tests could be run against the new, changed code.

Almost everything needs to be tested and automated. There are even ideologies such as **test-driven development (TDD)** and **behavior-driven development (BDD)**. If we don't write automated tests, our ever-changing code tends to break over time and becomes even harder to test and maintain.

In this chapter, we won't be talking about why we need to test our code. We'll accept that this is mandatory and is part of our life as programmers. We'll learn how to test the code written using RxJava.

We will see that it is not so hard to write unit tests for it, but that there are some hard-to-test cases, such as *asynchronous* Observable instances, for example. We will learn about some new operators, which will help us in testing and a new kind of Observable instance.

With that said, here is what we will cover in this chapter:

- Testing Observable instances via the BlockingObservable class and *aggregating* operators
- Using the TestSubscriber instance for in-depth testing
- The TestScheduler class and testing *asynchronous* Observable instances

Testing using simple subscription

We can test what we get by simply subscribing to the *source* Observable instance and collecting all of the incoming notifications. In order to demonstrate that, we'll develop a factory method for creating a new Observable instance and will test its behavior.

The method will receive a Comparator instance and multiple items, and will return Observable instance, emitting these items as a sorted sequence. The items will be sorted according to the Comparator instance passed.

We can develop the method using TDD. Let's first define the test as follows:

```java
public class SortedObservableTest {
  private Observable<String> tested;
  private List<String> expected;
  @Before
  public void before() {
    tested = CreateObservable.<String>sorted(
      (a, b) -> a.compareTo(b),
      "Star", "Bar", "Car", "War", "Far", "Jar");
    expected = Arrays.asList(
      "Bar", "Car", "Far", "Jar", "Star", "War"
    );
  }
  TestData data = new TestData();
  tested.subscribe(
    (v) -> data.getResult().add(v),
    (e) -> data.setError(e),
    () -> data.setCompleted(true)
  );
  Assert.assertTrue(data.isCompleted());
  Assert.assertNull(data.getError());
  Assert.assertEquals(expected, data.getResult());
}
```

 The examples of this chapter use the **JUnit** framework for testing. You can find out more about this at http://junit.org.

The test uses two variables to store the predefined reusable state. The first one is the Observable instance we use as source—tested. In the setup @Before method, it is assigned to the result of our method CreateObservable.sorted(Comparator, T...), which is not implemented yet. We compare a set of String instances and expect them to be received in the order they are stored in the *expected* variable—the second reusable field.

The test itself is quite verbose. It uses an instance of the `TestData` class to store the notifications incoming from the *tested* `Observable` instances.

If there is an `OnCompleted` notification, the `data.completed` field is set to `True`. We expect this to happen, and that's why we assert it at the end of the test method. If there is an `OnError` notification, the `data.error` field is set to the error. We don't expect that to happen, so we assert it to be `null`.

Every incoming item emitted by the `Observable` instances is added to the `data.resultList` field. At the end, it should be equal to the *expected* `List` variable, and we assert that.

 The source code for the preceding test can be viewed/downloaded at https://github.com/meddle0x53/learning-rxjava/blob/master/src/test/java/com/packtpub/reactive/chapter07/SortedObservableTest.java—this is the first test method.

However, this test fails, of course, because the `CreateObservable.sorted(Comparator, T...)` method is not implemented yet. Let's implement it and run the test again:

```
@SafeVarargs
public static <T> Observable<T> sorted(
  Comparator<? super T> comparator,
  T... data) {
    List<T> listData = Arrays.asList(data);
    listData.sort(comparator);
  return Observable.from(listData);
}
```

It's that simple! It just turns the passed `varargs` array into a `List` variable and uses its `sort()` method to sort it with the passed `Comparator` instance. Then, using the `Observable.from(Iterable)` method, we return the desired `Observable` instance.

 The source code for the preceding implementation can be found at: https://github.com/meddle0x53/learning-rxjava/blob/master/src/main/java/com/packtpub/reactive/common/CreateObservable.java#L262.

If we run the test now, it will pass. This is good! We've got our first test! But writing tests similar to this requires a lot of boilerplate code. We always need these three state variables and we always need to assert the same things. And what about *asynchronous* `Observable` instances, such as the ones created by `interval()` and `timer()` methods?

There are some techniques for removing the boilerplate variables, and later, we'll look at how to test *asynchronous* behavior as well. For now, we'll introduce one new type of observable.

The BlockingObservable class

Every `Observable` instance can be turned into a `BlockingObservable` instance with the `toBlocking()` method. The `BlockingObservable` instance has multiple methods that block the current thread, while everything is emitted by the *source* `Observable` instance until an `OnCompleted` or `OnError` notification is sent. If there is an `OnError` notification, an exception will be thrown (`RuntimeException` exceptions are thrown directly and checked exceptions are wrapped inside the `RuntimeException` instances).

The `toBlocking()` method doesn't block by itself, but the methods of the `BlockingObservable` instance it returns may block. Let's look at some of those methods:

- We can iterate over all the items in the `BlockingObservable` instance, using the `forEach()` method. Here is an example of using this:

```
Observable
    .interval(100L, TimeUnit.MILLISECONDS)
    .take(5)
    .toBlocking()
    .forEach(System.out::println);
System.out.println("END");
```

This is also an example of how to make *asynchronous* code behave *synchronously*. The `Observable` instance created by the `interval()` method will not execute in the background, because the `toBlocking()` method makes the current thread wait until it finishes. That's why we use the `take(int)` method here because, otherwise, the *main* thread would be blocked forever. The `forEach()` method will print the five items using the passed function and only after that will we see the END output. The `BlockingObservable` class has a `toIterable()` method too. The `Iterable` instance returned by it can be used for iterating over the sequence emitted by the source as well.

- There are *blocking* methods similar to *asynchronous*, such as `first()`, `last()`, `firstOrDefault()`, and `lastOrDefault()` methods (we talked about them in *Chapter 4, Transforming, Filtering, and Accumulating Your Data*). All of them block while waiting for the required item. Let's take a look at the following code snippet:

```
Integer first = Observable
  .range(3, 13).toBlocking().first();
  System.out.println(first);
  Integer last = Observable
  .range(3, 13).toBlocking().last();
  System.out.println(last);
```

This will print '3' and '15'.

- An interesting method is the `single()` method; it returns one item only when exactly one item is emitted by the *source* and the *source completes*. If there is no item emitted, or the *source* emits more than one item, a `NoSuchElementException` exception or an `IllegalArgumentException` exception is thrown, respectively.

- There is a `next()` method that doesn't *block* and instead returns an `Iterable` instance. When an `Iterator` instance is retrieved from this `Iterable` instance, each of its `next()` methods will *block*, while awaiting the next incoming item. This can be used on infinite `Observable` instances because the *current thread* will *block* only while waiting for the *next* item and then it will be able to continue. (Note that if no one calls the `next()` method in time, source elements may be skipped). Here is an example of using this:

```
Iterable<Long> next = Observable
  .interval(100L, TimeUnit.MILLISECONDS)
  .toBlocking()
  .next();
Iterator<Long> iterator = next.iterator();
System.out.println(iterator.next());
System.out.println(iterator.next());
System.out.println(iterator.next());
```

The *current thread* will *block* three times for 100 milliseconds and 0, 1, and 2 will be printed after every pause. There is a similar method called `latest()`, which returns an `Iterable` instance. The behavior is different because the `Iterable` instance produced by the `latest()` method returns the very last items emitted by the source or waits for the next ones, if there aren't any.

```
Iterable<Long> latest = Observable
    .interval(1000L, TimeUnit.MILLISECONDS)
    .toBlocking()
    .latest();
iterator = latest.iterator();
System.out.println(iterator.next());
Thread.sleep(5500L);
System.out.println(iterator.next());
System.out.println(iterator.next());
```

This will print 0 and then 5 and 6.

> The source code demonstrating all the preceding operators as well as the aggregate ones can be viewed/downloaded at https://github.com/meddle0x53/learning-rxjava/blob/master/src/main/java/com/packtpub/reactive/chapter07/BlockingObservablesAndOperators.java.

Using the `BlockingObservable` instances can help us collect our test data. But there is a set of `Observable` operators called **aggregate operators**, which, when combined with the `BlockingObservables` instances, are useful too.

The aggregate operators and the BlockingObservable class

Aggregate operators produce the `Observable` instances, which emit only one item and complete. This item is composed or is computed using all the items emitted by the *source* `Observable` instance. In this section, we'll talk about only two of them. For more detailed information, refer to https://github.com/ReactiveX/RxJava/wiki/Mathematical-and-Aggregate-Operators.

The first of these operators is the `count()` or `countLong()` method. It emits the number of the items emitted by the *source* `Observable` instance. For example:

```
Observable
    .range(10, 100)
    .count()
    .subscribe(System.out::println);
```

This will print `100`.

The other one is the `toList()` or `toSortedList()` method, which emits a `list` variable (that can be sorted) containing all of the items emitted by the *source* `Observable` instance and completes.

```
List<Integer> list = Observable
    .range(5, 15)
    .toList()
    .subscribe(System.out::println);
```

This will output the following:

```
[5, 6, 7, 8, 9, 10, 11, 12, 13, 14, 15, 16, 17, 18, 19]
```

All these methods, combined with the `toBlocking()` method, work well together. For example, if we want to retrieve the list of all the items emitted by the *source* `Observable` instance, we can do it like this:

```
List<Integer> single = Observable
    .range(5, 15)
    .toList()
    .toBlocking().single();
```

And we can use this collection of items however we want: for example, for testing.

> The aggregate operators include a `collect()` operator as well, which can be used for generating `Observable` instances and emitting arbitrary collections, say `Set()` operator, for example.

Testing with the aggregate operators and the BlockingObservable class

Using the operators and methods learned in the previous two sections, we are able to rework the test we've written to look like this:

```
@Test
public void testUsingBlockingObservable() {
  List<String> result = tested
    .toList()
    .toBlocking()
    .single();
  Assert.assertEquals(expected, result);
}
```

There is no boilerplate code here. We retrieve all the items emitted as a list and compare them to the expected list.

Using the `BlockingObsevables` class and the aggregate operators is pretty useful in most cases. While testing *asynchronous* `Observable` instances, which emit long, slow sequences, they are not so useful though. It is not good practice to block the test cases for a long time: slow tests are bad tests.

 The source code for the preceding test can be found at `https://github.com/meddle0x53/learning-rxjava/blob/master/src/test/java/com/packtpub/reactive/chapter07/SortedObservableTest.java` — this is the second test method.

Another case in which this method of testing is not helpful is when we want to inspect the `Notification` objects sent by the *source* or the subscription state.

There is one other technique for writing tests that gives us more fine-grained control over the *subscription* itself, and this is via a special `Subscriber` — the `TestSubscriber`.

Using the TestSubscriber class for in-depth testing

The `TestSubscriber` instance is a special `Subscriber` instance, which we can pass to the `subscribe()` method of any `Observable` instance.

We can retrieve all the received items and notifications from it. We can also look at the last `thread` on which the notifications have been received and the subscription state.

Let's rewrite our test using it, in order to demonstrate its capabilities and what it stores:

```
@Test
public void testUsingTestSubscriber() {
  TestSubscriber<String> subscriber =
    new TestSubscriber<String>();
  tested.subscribe(subscriber);
  Assert.assertEquals(expected, subscriber.getOnNextEvents());
  Assert.assertSame(1, subscriber.getOnCompletedEvents().size());
  Assert.assertTrue(subscriber.getOnErrorEvents().isEmpty());
  Assert.assertTrue(subscriber.isUnsubscribed());
}
```

The test is, again, very simple. We create a `TestSubscriber` instance and *subscribe* to the *tested* `Observable` instance with it. And we have access to the whole state after the `Observable` instance is *completed*. Let's take a look at the following term list:

- With the `getOnNextEvents()` method, we are able to retrieve all the items emitted by the `Observable` instance and compare them to the *expected* `List` variable.

- With the `getOnCompletedEvents()` method, we are able to inspect the *OnCompleted* notification and to check if it was sent at all. For example, the `Observable.never()` method doesn't send it.

- With the `getOnErrorEvents()` method, we are able to inspect *OnError* notifications if there were any. In this case, we *assert* that there were no *errors*.

- Using the `isUnsubscribed()` method, we can *assert* that, after everything *completed*, our `Subscriber` instances were *unsubscribed*.

The `TestSubscriber` instance has some *assertion* methods too. So, there is one more way in which the test could be written:

```
@Test
public void testUsingTestSubscriberAssertions() {
    TestSubscriber<String> subscriber = new
    TestSubscriber<String>();
    tested.subscribe(subscriber);
    subscriber.assertReceivedOnNext(expected);
    subscriber.assertTerminalEvent();
    subscriber.assertNoErrors();
    subscriber.assertUnsubscribed();
}
```

These are almost the same *assertions*, but done with the `TestSubscriber` instance's own `assert*` methods.

 The source code for the preceding test can be found at `https://github.com/meddle0x53/learning-rxjava/blob/master/src/test/java/com/packtpub/reactive/chapter07/SortedObservableTest.java` — these are the third and the fourth test methods.

With these techniques, we can test different behaviors and states of our `RxJava` logic. There is one last thing left to learn in this chapter — testing *asynchronous* `Observable` instances, such as the ones created by the `Observable.interval()` method.

Testing asynchronous Observable instances with the help of the TestScheduler class

There is one last type of predefined `scheduler` that we didn't mention in *Chapter 6, Using Concurrency and Parallelism with Schedulers*. This is the `TestScheduler` scheduler, a `scheduler` designed to be used in unit tests. All the actions scheduled on it are wrapped in objects containing the time they should be executed at, and won't be executed before the `triggerActions()` method of the `Scheduler` instance is called. This method executes all of the actions that are not executed and are scheduled to be executed at or before the `Scheduler` instance's present time. This time is virtual. This means that it is set by us and we can advance to any moment in the future using the special methods of this `scheduler`.

In order to demonstrate it, we'll want to develop another method for creating a new type of `observable`. The implementation of the method itself won't be discussed in this chapter, but you can find it in the source code accompanying the book.

The method creates an `Observable` instance emitting items at set time intervals. But the intervals are not equally spaced, such as with the built-in `interval` method. The idea is that we can provide a list of different multiple *intervals* and the `Observable` instance will cycle through it infinitely. The signature of the method is as follows:

```
Observable<Long> interval(List<Long> gaps, TimeUnit unit,
Scheduler scheduler)
```

Its behavior should be the same as that of the `Observable.interval` method if we pass a `List` variable containing only one time period value. And here is the test for this case:

```
@Test
public void testBehavesAsNormalIntervalWithOneGap() {
  TestScheduler testScheduler = Schedulers.test(); // (1)
  Observable<Long> interval = CreateObservable.interval(
    Arrays.asList(100L), TimeUnit.MILLISECONDS, testScheduler
  ); // (2)
  TestSubscriber<Long> subscriber = new TestSubscriber<Long>();
  interval.subscribe(subscriber); // (3)
  assertTrue(subscriber.getOnNextEvents().isEmpty()); // (4)
  testScheduler.advanceTimeBy(101L, TimeUnit.MILLISECONDS); // (5)
  assertEquals(Arrays.asList(0L), subscriber.getOnNextEvents());
  testScheduler.advanceTimeBy(101L, TimeUnit.MILLISECONDS); // (6)
  assertEquals(
    Arrays.asList(0L, 1L),
    subscriber.getOnNextEvents()
  );
  testScheduler.advanceTimeTo(1L, TimeUnit.SECONDS); // (7)
  assertEquals(
    Arrays.asList(0L, 1L, 2L, 3L, 4L, 5L, 6L, 7L, 8L, 9L),
    subscriber.getOnNextEvents()
  );
}
```

Let's take a look at the following explaination:

1. We create the TestScheduler instance, using the Schedulers.test() method.

2. Our method receives a Scheduler instance as its third parameter. It will *emit items* on it, so we pass our TestScheduler instance.

3. Using a TestSubscriber instance, we *subscribe* to the Observable instance.

4. Immediately after subscribing, we shouldn't have any notifications, so we check that.

5. The TestScheduler instance has an advanceTimeBy(long, TimeUnit) method, which controls the time of its Worker instances, so we can use it to get 101 milliseconds into the future. After 101 milliseconds, we expect to have received one item — 0.

6. Using the advanceTimeBy() method, we advance 101 more milliseconds into the future, and we should have received 0 and 1.

7. The other important method of the TestScheduler instance is the advanceTimeTo(long, TimeUnit) method. It can be used to advance to a specific time point in the future. So we use it to get to the moment when exactly one second from the *subscription* has passed. We expect to have received ten notifications by that time.

The TestScheduler instance controls the time using its advanceTimeBy() and advanceTimeTo() methods, so we don't need to *block* the *main* Thread instance waiting for something to happen. We can just go to the time it has already happened. With the TestScheduler instance, there is a global order of events. So, if two tasks are scheduled for the exact same time, they have an order in which they will execute and can cause problems with the test that expect a specific global order. If we have such an operator to test, we should avoid this by timing to different values — one to 100 ms and the other to 101 ms. Using this technique, testing *asynchronous* Observable instances is not such a complex task anymore.

 The source code for the preceding test can be found at: https://github.com/meddle0x53/learning-rxjava/blob/master/src/test/java/com/packtpub/reactive/chapter07/CreateObservableIntervalTest.java.

Summary

With this chapter, not only did we find out how to write programs using RxJava, but we also saw how to test any aspect of them. We've learned about a few new operators and the `BlockingObservables` class too.

The RxJava library has many operators that are not mentioned in this book, but we've studied the more important and useful ones. You can always refer to `https://github.com/ReactiveX/RxJava/wiki` for the rest. There is also much more regarding *subscriptions*, *backpressure*, and the `Observable` instance *life cycle*, but with your current knowledge, it won't be hard to master everything in the library. Remember that this is just a library, a tool to write code. The logic is the important thing here. This way of programming is somewhat different from the procedural one, but once you get into it, it feels natural.

In the next and final chapter, we will learn how to free resources allocated by *subscriptions*, how to prevent memory leaks, and how to create our own operators that can be chained in the `RxJava` logic.

8
Resource Management and Extending RxJava

Through the previous chapters, we've learned how to use RxJava's observables. We've been using many different operators and `factory` methods. The `factory` methods were the source of various `Observable` instances with different behavior and origin of their emissions. Using the operators, on the other hand, we've been building complex logic around these observables.

In this chapter, we'll learn how to create our own `factory` methods, which will be capable of managing their source resources. In order to do that, we'll need a way to manage and dispose of the resources. We've created and used multiple methods like this with source files, HTTP requests, folders, or data in the memory. But some of them don't clean up their resources. For example, the HTTP request observable needs a `CloseableHttpAsyncClient` instance; we created a method that receives it and left the management of it to the user. The time has come to learn how to manage and clean up our source data automatically, encapsulated in our `factory` methods.

We'll learn how to write our own operators, too. Java is not a dynamic language, and that's why we won't be adding operators as methods of the `Observable` class. There is a way to insert them in the observable chain of actions and we will see that in this chapter.

The topics covered in this chapter are:

- Resource management with the `using()` method
- Creating custom operators using the *higher-order* `lift()` operator
- Creating compositions of operators with `compose`

Resource management

If we look back at the HTTP request method that we used in *Chapter 6,*
Using Concurrency and Parallelism with Schedulers and *Chapter 5, Combinators,*
Conditionals, and Error Handling, it has this signature: `Observable<Map>`
`requestJson(HttpAsyncClient client, String url)`.

Instead of just calling a method that makes a request to a URL and returns the
response as JSON, we create a `HttpAsyncClient` instance, have to start the it and
pass it to the `requestJson()` method. But there is more: we need to close the *client*
after we read the result, and because the observable is *asynchronous*, we need to wait
for its `OnCompleted` notification and then to do the closing. This is very complex
and should be changed. The `Observable`, which read from files, need to create
streams/readers/channels and close them when all the subscribers are *unsubscribed*.
The `Observable`, emitting data from a database should set up and then close all the
connections, statements, and result sets that are used after reading is done. And that
is true for the `HttpAsyncClient` object, too. It is the resource that we use to open a
connection to a remote server; our observable should clean it up after everything is
read and all the subscribers are no longer subscribed.

Let's answer this one question: Why does the `requestJson()` method need this
`HttpAsyncClient` object? The answer is that we used a RxJava module for the HTTP
request. The code for this is as follows:

```
ObservableHttp
  .createGet(url, client)
  .toObservable();
```

This code creates the request and the code needs the client, so we need the client
to create our `Observable` instance. We can't change this code, because changing
it means to write the HTTP request by ourselves, and that's not good. There is
already a library that does it for us. We'll have to use something that provides the
`HttpAsyncClient` instance on *subscribing* and disposes from it on *unsubscribing*.
There is something that does just this: the `using()` factory method.

Introducing the Observable.using method

The signature of the `Observable.using` method is as follows:

```
public final static <T, Resource> Observable<T> using(
  final Func0<Resource> resourceFactory,
  final Func1<? super Resource, ? extends Observable<? extends T>>
  observableFactory,
  final Action1<? super Resource> disposeAction
)
```

This looks quite complex, but after a second glance it is not so hard to understand. Let's take a look at the following description:

- Its first parameter is `Func0<Resource> resourceFactory`, a function that creates a `Resource` object (here `Resource` is an arbitrary object; it is not interface or class but the name of a type parameter). It is our job to implement the resource creation.

- The `Func1<? super Resource, ? extends Observable<? extends T>> observableFactory` parameter, the second argument, is a function that receives a `Resource` object and returns an `Observable` instance. This function will be called with the `Resource` object that we already created by the first parameter. We can use this resource to create our `Observable` instance.

- The `Action1<? super Resource> disposeAction` parameter is called when the `Resource` object should be disposed of. It receives the `Resource` object that was created by the `resourceFactory` parameter (and used to create an `Observable` instance), and it is our job to dispose of it. This is called on *unsubscribing*.

We are able to create a function, making an HTTP request, without passing it the `HttpAsyncClient` object now. We have utilities that will create and dispose of it on demand. Let's implement the function:

```
// (1)
public Observable<ObservableHttpResponse> request(String url) {
  Func0<CloseableHttpAsyncClient> resourceFactory = () -> {
    CloseableHttpAsyncClient client =
    HttpAsyncClients.createDefault(); // (2)
    client.start();
    System.out.println(
      Thread.currentThread().getName() +
      " : Created and started the client."
    );
    return client;
  };
  Func1<HttpAsyncClient, Observable<ObservableHttpResponse>>
  observableFactory = (client) -> { // (3)
    System.out.println(
      Thread.currentThread().getName() + " : About to create
      Observable."
    );
    return ObservableHttp.createGet(url, client).toObservable();
  };
  Action1<CloseableHttpAsyncClient> disposeAction = (client) -> {
    try { // (4)
```

```
            System.out.println(
                Thread.currentThread().getName() + " : Closing the
                client."
            );
            client.close();
        }
        catch (IOException e) {}
    };
    return Observable.using( // (5)
        resourceFactory,
        observableFactory,
        disposeAction
    );
}
```

The method is not so hard to understand. Let's break it down:

1. The signature of the method is simple; it has only one parameter, URL. The callers of the method won't need to create and manage the life cycle of a CloseableHttpAsyncClient instance. It returns an Observable instance capable of emitting a ObservableHttpResponse response and *completing*. The getJson() method can use that to transform the ObservableHttpResponse response into the Map instance representing the JSON, again without the need of passing the *client*.

2. The resourceFactory lambda is simple; it creates a default CloseableHttpAsyncClient instance and starts it. When called, it will return an initialized HTTP *client* capable of requesting remote server data. We output that the *client* is ready for debugging purposes.

3. The observableFactory function has access to the CloseableHttpAsyncClient instance that was created by the resourceFactory function, so it uses it and the passed URL to construct the resulting Observable instance. This is done through RxJava's rxjava-apache-http module API (https://github.com/ReactiveX/RxApacheHttp). We output what we are doing.

4. The disposeAction function receives the CloseableHttpAsyncClient object that was used for the creation of the Observable instance and *closes* it. Again, we print a message to the standard output that we are about to do that.

5. With the help of the using() factory method, we return our HTTP *request* Observable instance. This won't trigger any of the three lambdas yet. *Subscribing* to the returned Observable instance will call the resourceFactory function, and then the observableFactory function.

This is how we implemented an `Observable` instance capable of managing its own resources. Let's see how it is used:

```
String url = "https://api.github.com/orgs/ReactiveX/repos";

Observable<ObservableHttpResponse> response = request(url);

System.out.println("Not yet subscribed.");

Observable<String> stringResponse = response
.<String>flatMap(resp -> resp.getContent()
.map(bytes -> new String(bytes, java.nio.charset.StandardCharsets.
UTF_8))
.retry(5)

.map(String::trim);

System.out.println("Subscribe 1:");
System.out.println(stringResponse.toBlocking().first());

System.out.println("Subscribe 2:");
System.out.println(stringResponse.toBlocking().first());
```

We use the new `request()` method to list the repositories of the *ReactiveX orgranisation*. We just pass the URL to it and we get an `Observable` response. Until we subscribe to it, no resources will be allocated and no requests will be executed, so we print that you are not yet subscribed.

The `stringResponse` observable contains logic and converts the raw `ObservableHttpResponse` object to `String`. Still, no resources are allocated and no request is sent.

We use the `BlockingObservable` class' `first()` method to subscribe to the `Observable` instance and wait for its result. We retrieve the response as `String` and output it. Now, a resource is allocated and a request is made. After the data is fetched, the `subscriber` encapsulated by the `BlockingObservable` instance is automatically unsubscribed, so the resource used (the HTTP client) is disposed of. We make a second subscription in order to see what happens next.

Let's look at the output of this program:

```
Not yet subscribed.
Subscribe 1:
main : Created and started the client.
main : About to create Observable.
[{"id":7268616,"name":"Rx.rb","full_name":"ReactiveX/Rx.rb",...
```

```
Subscribe 2:
I/O dispatcher 1 : Closing the client.
main : Created and started the client.
main : About to create Observable.
I/O dispatcher 5 : Closing the client.
[{"id":7268616,"name":"Rx.rb","full_name":"ReactiveX/Rx.rb",...
```

So, when we subscribe to the website, the HTTP client and the `Observable` instances are created, using our factory lambdas. The creation is executed on the current main thread. The request is made and printed (cropped here). The client is disposed of on an IO thread and the request is executed when the `Observable` instance completes the execution.

When subscribing for the second time, we go through the same process from the beginning; we allocate the resource, create `Observable` instance and dispose of the resource. This is because the `using()` method works that way — it allocates one resource per subscription. We can use different techniques to reuse the same result on the next subscription instead of making a new request and allocating resource for it. For example, we can reuse the `CompositeSubscription` method for multiple subscribers or a `Subject` instance. However, there is one easier way to reuse the fetched response of the next subscription.

Caching data with Observable.cache

We can use caching to cache the response in the memory and then, on the next subscription, instead of requesting the remote server again, to use the cached data.

Let's change the code to look like this:

```
String url = "https://api.github.com/orgs/ReactiveX/repos";
Observable<ObservableHttpResponse> response = request(url);

System.out.println("Not yet subscribed.");
Observable<String> stringResponse = response
.flatMap(resp -> resp.getContent()
.map(bytes -> new String(bytes)))
.retry(5)
.cast(String.class)
.map(String::trim)
.cache();

System.out.println("Subscribe 1:");
System.out.println(stringResponse.toBlocking().first());

System.out.println("Subscribe 2:");
System.out.println(stringResponse.toBlocking().first());
```

The cache() operator called at the end of the stringResponse chain will cache the response represented by a string for all the following subscribers. So, the output this time will be:

```
Not yet subscribed.
Subscribe 1:
main : Created and started the client.
main : About to create Observable.
[{"id":7268616,"name":"Rx.rb",...
I/O dispatcher 1 : Closing the client.
Subscribe 2:
[{"id":7268616,"name":"Rx.rb",...
```

Now, we can reuse our stringResponse Observable instance through our programs without making additional resource allocation and request.

> The demo source code can be found at https://github.com/
> meddle0x53/learning-rxjava/blob/master/src/main/java/
> com/packtpub/reactive/chapter08/ResourceManagement.
> java.

At last, the requestJson() method can be implemented like this:

```
public Observable<Map> requestJson(String url) {
Observable<String> rawResponse = request(url)

. . . .

return Observable.amb(fromCache(url), response);
}
```

Simpler and with resource auto management (the resource, a http client is created and destroyed automatically), the method implements its own caching functionality too (we implemented it back in *Chapter 5, Combinators, Conditionals, and Error Handling*).

> All the methods, which create Observable instances, developed through
> the book can be found at https://github.com/meddle0x53/
> learning-rxjava/blob/master/src/main/java/com/
> packtpub/reactive/common/CreateObservable.java class
> contained in the source code. There is also a cache-in-files implementation
> for the requestJson() method that you can find there.

With this, we are able to extend RxJava, creating our own factory methods to make `Observable` instances dependent on arbitrary data sources.

The next section of the chapter will show how to put our own logic into the `Observable` chain of operators.

Creating custom operators with lift

After learning about and using so many various operators, we are ready to write our own operators. The `Observable` class has an operator called `lift`. It receives an instance of the `Operator` interface. This interface is just an empty one that extends the `Func1<Subscriber<? super R>, Subscriber<? super T>>` interface. This means that we can pass even lambdas as operators.

The best way of learning how to use the `lift` operator is to write an example of it. Let's create an operator that adds a sequential index to every item emitted (of course, this is doable without a dedicated operator). This way, we will be able to produce indexed items. For this purpose, we need a class that stores an item and its index. Let's create a more general class called `Pair`:

```java
public class Pair<L, R> {
    final L left;
    final R right;

public Pair(L left, R right) {
    this.left = left;
    this.right = right;
    }

    public L getLeft() {
      return left;
    }

public R getRight() {
      return right;
    }

    @Override
    public String toString() {
       return String.format("%s : %s", this.left, this.right);
    }

    // hashCode and equals omitted

}'
```

The instances of this class are very simple *immutable* objects that contain two arbitrary objects. In our case, the *left* field will be the index of type Long and the *right* field will be the emitted item. The Pair class, as with any *immutable* class, contains implementations of the hashCode() and equals() methods.

Here is the code for the operator:

```
public class Indexed<T> implements Operator<Pair<Long, T>, T> {
  private final long initialIndex;
  public Indexed() {
    this(0L);
  }
  public Indexed(long initial) {
    this. initialIndex = initial;
  }
  @Override
  public Subscriber<? super T> call(Subscriber<? super Pair<Long, T>>
  s) {
    return new Subscriber<T>(s) {
      private long index = initialIndex;
      @Override
      public void onCompleted() {
        s.onCompleted();
      }
      @Override
      public void onError(Throwable e) {
        s.onError(e);
      }
      @Override
      public void onNext(T t) {
        s.onNext(new Pair<Long, T>(index++, t));
      }
    };
  }
}
```

The call() method of the Operator interface has one parameter, a Subscriber instance. This instance will subscribe to the observable that will be returned by the lift() operator. The method returns a new Subscriber instance, which will subscribe to the observable upon which the lift() operator was called. We can change the data of all the notifications in it and that is how we will be writing our own operator's logic.

The `Indexed` class has a state—index. By default, its initial value is 0, but there is a *constructor* that can create an `Indexed` instance with arbitrary initial value. Our operator delegates the `OnError` and `OnCompleted` notifications to the subscribers unchanged. The interesting method is `onNext()`. It modifies the incoming item by creating a `Pair` instance of it and the current value of `index` field. After that, the `index` is incremented. That way, the next item will use the incremented `index` and increment it again.

And now, we have our first operator. Let's write an unit test to showcase its behavior:

```
@Test
public void testGeneratesSequentialIndexes() {
  Observable<Pair<Long, String>> observable = Observable
    .just("a", "b", "c", "d", "e")
    .lift(new Indexed<String>());
  List<Pair<Long, String>> expected = Arrays.asList(
    new Pair<Long, String>(0L, "a"),
    new Pair<Long, String>(1L, "b"),
    new Pair<Long, String>(2L, "c"),
    new Pair<Long, String>(3L, "d"),
    new Pair<Long, String>(4L, "e")
  );
  List<Pair<Long, String>> actual = observable
    .toList()
    .toBlocking().
    single();
  assertEquals(expected, actual);
  // Assert that it is the same result for a second subscribtion.
  TestSubscriber<Pair<Long, String>> testSubscriber = new
  TestSubscriber<Pair<Long, String>>();
  observable.subscribe(testSubscriber);
  testSubscriber.assertReceivedOnNext(expected);
}
```

The test emits the letters from 'a' to 'e' and uses the `lift()` operator to insert our `Indexed` operator implementation into the observable chain. We expect a list of five `Pair` instances of sequential numbers starting from zero—the *indexes* and the letters. We use the `toList().toBlocking().single()` technique to retrieve the actual list of emitted items and to assert that they are equal to the expected emissions. Because `Pair` instances have the `hashCode()` and `equals()` methods defined, we can compare `Pair` instances, so the test passes. If we *subscribe* for the second time, the `Indexed` operator should provide indexing from the initial index, 0. Using a `TestSubscriber` instance, we do that and assert that the letters are indexed, starting with 0.

> The code for the Indexed operator can be found at https://github.
> com/meddle0x53/learning-rxjava/blob/master/src/main/
> java/com/packtpub/reactive/chapter08/Lift.java and the
> unit test testing its behavior at https://github.com/meddle0x53/
> learning-rxjava/blob/master/src/test/java/com/
> packtpub/reactive/chapter08/IndexedTest.java.

Using the `lift()` operator and different `Operator` implementations, we can write our own operators, which operate on every single item of the emitted sequence. But in most cases, we will be able to implement our logic without creating new operators. For example, the indexed behavior can be implemented in many different ways, one of which is by *zipping* with `Observable.range` method, like this:

```
Observable<Pair<Long, String>> indexed = Observable.zip(
  Observable.just("a", "b", "c", "d", "e"),
  Observable.range(0, 100),
  (s, i) -> new Pair<Long, String>((long) i, s)
);
subscribePrint(indexed, "Indexed, no lift");
```

Implementing a new operator has many traps, such as chaining the subscriptions, supporting *backpressure*, and reusing variables. If possible, we should try to compose the existing operators, which are written by experienced RxJava contributors. So, in some cases, an operator that transforms the `Observable` itself is a better idea, for example, applying multiple operators on it as one. For this, we can use the *composing* operator, `compose()`.

Composing multiple operators with the Observable.compose operator

The `compose()` operator has one parameter of type `Transformer`. The `Transformer` interface, like the `Operator` one, is an *empty* interface that extends `Func1` (this approach hides the type complexities that are involved by using `Func1`). The difference is that it extends the `Func1<Observable<T>, Observable<R>>` method, so that it transforms an `Observable` and not a `Subscriber`. This means that, instead of operating on each individual item emitted by the *source* observable, it operates directly on the source.

We can illustrate the use of this operator and the `Transformer` interface through an example. First, we will create a `Transformer` implementation:

```
public class OddFilter<T> implements Transformer<T, T> {
  @Override
  public Observable<T> call(Observable<T> observable) {
    return observable
      .lift(new Indexed<T>(1L))
      .filter(pair -> pair.getLeft() % 2 == 1)
      .map(pair -> pair.getRight());
  }
}
```

The idea of this implementation is to filter the emissions of an observable, depending on the order in which they are incoming. It operates on the whole sequence, using our `Indexed` operator to add an index to every item. After that, it filters the `Pair` instances that have odd indexes and retrieves the original items from the filtered `Pair` instances. That way, only the members of the emitted sequence that are placed at odd positions reach the subscribers.

Again let's write a *unit test*, ensuring that the new `OddFilter` transformer behaves in the right way:

```
@Test
public void testFiltersOddOfTheSequence() {
  Observable<String> tested = Observable
    .just("One", "Two", "Three", "Four", "Five", "June", "July")
    .compose(new OddFilter<String>());
  List<String> expected =
    Arrays.asList("One", "Three", "Five", "July");
  List<String> actual = tested
    .toList()
    .toBlocking()
    .single();
  assertEquals(expected, actual);
}
```

As you can see, an instance of our `OddFilter` class is passed to the `compose()` operator, and that way, it is applied to the observable that was created by the `range()` factory method. The observable emits seven strings. If the `OddFilter` implementation works right, it should filter out the strings emitted at odd positions.

The source code of the OddFilter class can be found at `https://github.com/meddle0x53/learning-rxjava/blob/master/src/main/java/com/packtpub/reactive/chapter08/Compose.java`. The unit test testing it can be viewed/downloaded at `https://github.com/meddle0x53/learning-rxjava/blob/master/src/test/java/com/packtpub/reactive/chapter08/IndexedTest.java`.

More about implementing custom operators can be found here: `https://github.com/ReactiveX/RxJava/wiki/Implementing-Your-Own-Operators`. If you use RxJava in dynamic languages such Groovy, you'll be able to extend the `Observable` class with new methods, or you can use RxJava with Xtend, a flexible dialect of Java. Refer to `http://mnmlst-dvlpr.blogspot.de/2014/07/rxjava-and-xtend.html`.

Summary

Creating our own operators and resource-dependent `Observable` instances gives us unlimited possibilities when it comes to creating logic around the `Observable` class. We are able to turn each data source into an `Observable` instance and transform the incoming data in many different ways.

I wanted this book to cover the most interesting and important parts of RxJava. If I have missed something important, the documentation at `https://github.com/ReactiveX/RxJava/wiki` is one of the best on the web.. Refer especially to this section for further reading: `https://github.com/ReactiveX/RxJava/wiki/Additional-Reading`.

I have tried to structure the code and the ideas and to provide them in small iterations over the chapters. The first and second chapters are more ideological; they introduce the reader to the basic ideas of the functional programming and the reactive programming and the second chapter tries to establish the the origins of the `Observable` class. The third chapter provides the reader with the means to create a variety of different `Observable` instances. The fourth and fifth chapters teach us how to write logic around those `Observable` instances and the sixth adds multi-threading to this logic. The seventh chapter comes with *unit testing* the logic that the reader has learned to write and the eight tries to extend the capabilities of this logic even further.

I hope you, the reader, found this book useful. Don't forget, RxJava is just a tool. The important things are your knowledge and your thinking.

Index

A

accumulator 71
aggregate operators
  about 132
  reference link 132
  used, for testing 134
  using 132, 133
amb operator
  about 83
  reference link 86
  using 84
Android module
  reference link 115
asynchronous Observable instances
  testing, with TestScheduler
    class 136-138

B

backpressure operators
  about 125
  reference link 125
behavior-driven development (BDD) 127
BlockingObservable class
  about 130
  using 130-132
  used, for testing 134
  with aggregate operators 132, 133
buffering 120, 121
buffer operator
  about 123
  using 123, 124

C

cast() operator
  about 64
  using 64
cold Observable instance 43
combineLatest operator
  used, for combining Observable
    instances 78, 79
concat operator
  used, for combining Observable
    instances 81, 82
conditional operators
  about 83
  amb operator 83, 84
  defaultIfEmpty() operator 86
  skipUntil() operator 84, 85
  skipWhile() operator 84, 85
  takeUntil() operator 84, 85
  takeWhile() operator 84, 85
ConnectableObservable class
  about 44
  using 45
custom operators
  creating, with lift operator 148-151
  reference link 153

D

data
  accumulating 71-73
  caching, with Observable.cache 146-148
  filtering 65-70

X

Xtend
  about 153
  reference link 153

Z

zip operator
  used, for combining Observable
      instances 76, 77

Thank you for buying
Learning Reactive Programming
with Java 8

About Packt Publishing

Packt, pronounced 'packed', published its first book, *Mastering phpMyAdmin for Effective MySQL Management*, in April 2004, and subsequently continued to specialize in publishing highly focused books on specific technologies and solutions.

Our books and publications share the experiences of your fellow IT professionals in adapting and customizing today's systems, applications, and frameworks. Our solution-based books give you the knowledge and power to customize the software and technologies you're using to get the job done. Packt books are more specific and less general than the IT books you have seen in the past. Our unique business model allows us to bring you more focused information, giving you more of what you need to know, and less of what you don't.

Packt is a modern yet unique publishing company that focuses on producing quality, cutting-edge books for communities of developers, administrators, and newbies alike. For more information, please visit our website at www.packtpub.com.

About Packt Open Source

In 2010, Packt launched two new brands, Packt Open Source and Packt Enterprise, in order to continue its focus on specialization. This book is part of the Packt Open Source brand, home to books published on software built around open source licenses, and offering information to anybody from advanced developers to budding web designers. The Open Source brand also runs Packt's Open Source Royalty Scheme, by which Packt gives a royalty to each open source project about whose software a book is sold.

Writing for Packt

We welcome all inquiries from people who are interested in authoring. Book proposals should be sent to author@packtpub.com. If your book idea is still at an early stage and you would like to discuss it first before writing a formal book proposal, then please contact us; one of our commissioning editors will get in touch with you.

We're not just looking for published authors; if you have strong technical skills but no writing experience, our experienced editors can help you develop a writing career, or simply get some additional reward for your expertise.

Please check **www.PacktPub.com** for information on our titles

www.ingramcontent.com/pod-product-compliance
Lightning Source LLC
Chambersburg PA
CBHW060134060326
40690CB00018B/3874